Eyewitness
Islam

A poetry reading

Seventh-century coin, minted when the Umayyad dynasty ruled from Damascus, Syria

Arabic quadrant, for measuring the height of stars, with instructions

Water pitcher presented to Charlemagne by eighth-century caliph, Harun al-Rashid

Mosque finial of Selimiye Mosque, Turkey

Lute decorated with traditional Islamic patterns

Star lantern

Map of the world by Moroccan-born writer and geographer, Al-Idrisi (1099–1180)

Guidebook to the *hajj* (the pilgrimage)

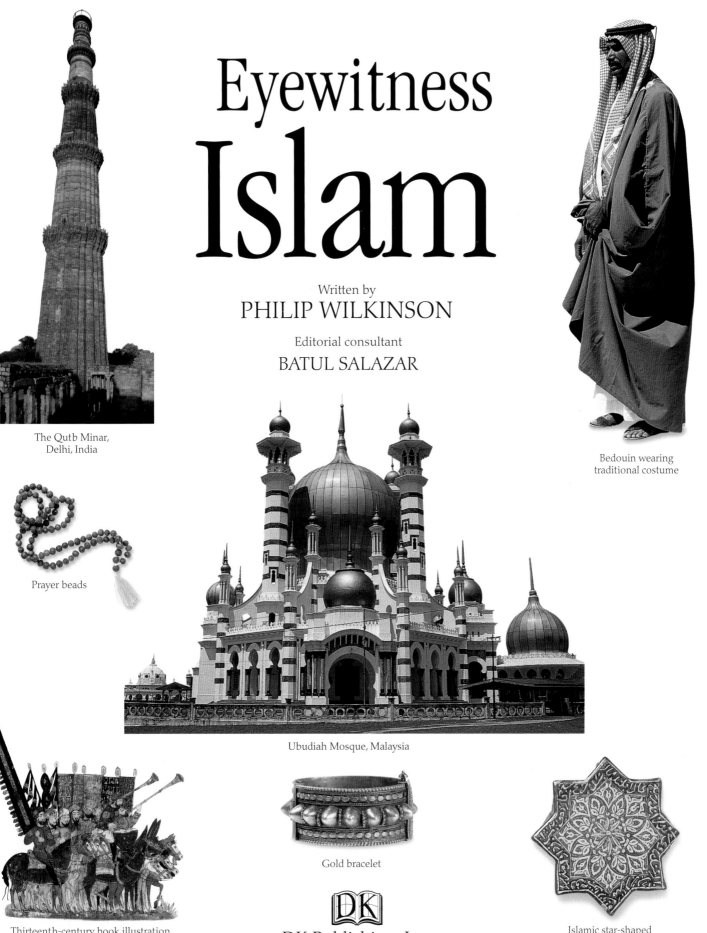

Eyewitness
Islam

Written by
PHILIP WILKINSON

Editorial consultant
BATUL SALAZAR

The Qutb Minar,
Delhi, India

Bedouin wearing
traditional costume

Prayer beads

Ubudiah Mosque, Malaysia

Gold bracelet

Thirteenth-century book illustration
of Ramadan procession

Islamic star-shaped
decorative tile

DK Publishing, Inc.

Sixteenth-century painting
of Muslim astronomers

Bronze bird from Persia

DK

LONDON, NEW YORK,
MELBOURNE, MUNICH, and DELHI

Project editor Kitty Blount
Art editor Clair Watson
Editor Fran Baines
Production Kate Oliver
Special photography Steve Teague
Picture research Angela Anderson, Alex Pepper,
Deborah Pownall, and Sarah Pownall
DTP designer Siu Yin Ho
Jacket designer Dean Price

REVISED EDITION

Editors Elizabeth Hester, Laura Buller
Publishing director Beth Sutinis
Art director Dirk Kaufman
DTP designer Milos Orlovic
Production Chris Avgherinos, Ivor Parker

This Eyewitness ® Guide has been conceived by
Dorling Kindersley Limited and Editions Gallimard

This edition published in the United States in 2005
by DK Publishing
345 Hudson Street, New York, NY 10014

14 15 10 9 8 7 6 5
007-ED310-Jul/2009

A catalog record for this book is
available from the Library of Congress.

ISBN 978-0-7566-1077-7 (Hardcover) 978-0-7566-1078-4 (Library Binding)

Color reproduction by
Colourscan, Singapore
Printed and bound in China by South China
Printing Co. Ltd

Saudi Arabian
woman wearing a
face veil

Traditional silk costume
from China

Two of the Rightly Guided Caliphs,
Companions of the Prophet

Tenth-century Arabic copy of a
herbal encyclopedia by Greek
surgeon Dioscorides

A book rest supporting
a copy of the Qur'an

A caravan of pilgrims, including a camel
carrying a pavillion called a *mahmal*.

Discover more at
www.dk.com

Coffeepot

Contents

Mamluk mosque lamp

Early Arabia

THE ARABIAN PENINSULA is home to the Arab people. There had already been advanced cultures in this area before the birth of Muhammad, the Prophet of Islam, in the sixth century. Arabia's position at a crossroads between Asia, Africa, and Europe allowed many Arabs to make fortunes trading. Although most of the Arab tribes worshiped their own idols, Christians, Jews, and followers of Abraham worshiped One God. When Muhammad told them that the religion of the One God had been revealed to him and that at last they had a message, the Qur'an, in their own language and a religion called Islam, some were enthusiastic.

SOUTH ARABIC INSCRIPTION
The Sabaeans, who ruled southern Arabia between the eighth and second centuries BCE, used a script called South Arabic. Archaeologists have found many inscriptions in this angular script, which passed out of use after the Sabaeans lost power.

DATE HARVEST
Settlements grew up at the small oases that are dotted around the Arabian Peninsula. Here there was a reliable water supply and date palms grew, providing a succulent harvest for the local people.

DESERT DUNES
Much of Arabia is desert – either vast expanses of sand with rolling dunes or the desert of black volcanic rocks around the city of Mecca. The name Arab means "nomad" because, in such an environment, many Arab people adopted a nomadic way of life in order to survive.

PETRIFIED FOREST
The Arabian Peninsula is, for the most part, an inhospitable terrain of desert and harsh landscapes, such as these jagged rocks. The most fertile area is Yemen, which gets monsoon rains from the Indian Ocean.

WOMAN FROM PALMYRA
The city of Palmyra in the Syrian desert was built where several trade routes met. Its people became rich because they charged merchants a tax when they passed through. This Palmyra woman is displaying her wealth in the form of gold jewelry.

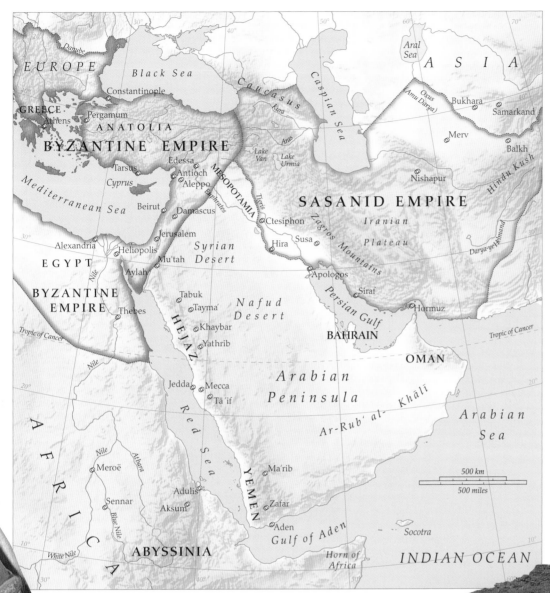

The Arab world at the time of the birth of the Prophet Muhammad in 570

THE ARAB WORLD
The Arabian Peninsula lies between the Red Sea and the Persian Gulf. The Arab peoples built towns in the fertile area of Yemen, at oases, and on the coasts. To the northeast, the Sasanid Empire of the Persians occupied Iran. To the northwest lay the Christian Byzantine Empire.

Altar for burning frankincense

PRECIOUS PERFUME
Frankincense was one of Arabia's most prized products, and it was widely traded. Trade routes criss-crossed the peninsula and many of the area's early cities, such as Ma'rib and the Nabatean town of Petra (in modern Jordan), grew up along the roads. Trade has been vital to the area ever since.

WALLS AT MA'RIB
Ma'rib, in Yemen, was the capital city of the Sabaeans, and some of its ancient walls survive. Ma'rib was built on a trade route and grew into a large, thriving city, with a palace (home of the Queen of Sheba) and many houses. There was also a famous dam, an amazing feat of engineering for the seventh century BCE.

The Prophet Muhammad

MUHAMMAD WAS BORN IN 570 in the city of Mecca (in what is now Saudi Arabia). He was a member of the Quraysh tribe. Orphaned as a boy, he was brought up by his grandfather and uncle. His mission as Prophet of Islam began in 610, when the Qur'an was first revealed to him. Three years later, Muhammad began to preach. He attracted some followers, but his teachings about the one God were not widely welcomed in Mecca, where most of the people worshiped idols, many different pagan gods. Eventually he moved to the city of Medina, which became the center of a great Islamic civilization.

ARCHANGEL GABRIEL
The Qur'an (pp. 10–11) was revealed to Muhammad by the archangel Gabriel, the angel of revelation. On an occasion known as the Night of Destiny, the revelation began. Then the Qur'an was communicated in small parts over a number of years.

WRITTEN OR SPOKEN
This calligraphy represents the name of the Prophet, Muhammad. According to tradition, he actually has 200 names, including Habib Allah (Beloved of God) and Miftah al-Jannah (Key of Paradise). When referring to Muhammad, Muslims usually add the phrase 'alayhi-s-salam (peace be upon him).

The word "Muhammad" written in calligraphy

THE LIFE OF A TRADER
As a young man, Muhammad became a merchant, working for a wealthy widow called Khadija. Arabia was crisscrossed with trading routes linking the peninsula with the Mediterranean and the Indian Ocean. Muhammad traveled with camel caravans along these routes and made several trading journeys as far as Syria. Khadija was impressed with Muhammad, and, although she was considerably older than he was, the two married.

JABAL AN-NUR
Jabal an-Nur (the Mountain of Light) a few miles from Mecca, is the place where Muhammad went to meditate. Every year, during the month of Ramadan (p. 15), Muhammad retired to the mountain to pray, fast, and give to the poor. It was on one of these retreats that the Prophet received the first revelation of the Qur'an.

THE PROPHET
Muhammad, whose name is shown here in stylized form, is the Prophet of Islam. Muslims see him as the last of a series of prophets, including Abraham, Moses, and Jesus, all of whom were mortal.

ON THE MOUNTAIN
When visiting Jabal an-Nur, Muhammad stayed in a cave called Hirah, at the top of the rocky peak. The cave, with an opening that faced toward Mecca, was very small, but there was enough space for Muhammad to pray. One of the Prophet's daughters used to climb the mountain to bring him food so that he could stay in the cave for the whole month of Ramadan.

ALLAH

Allah is the name of the one God in whom Muslims believe and upon whom all life and all existence depends. He is unique and infinitely greater than any thing He has created. The Qur'an says that He is "unbegotten." In other words, He is eternal, having no origin and no end. He is and always will be.

Star pattern based on "Allah" in Arabic script

The Prophet's mosque

MEDINA

Muhammad was persecuted in his native Mecca and some of his followers took refuge in Abyssinia (present-day Ethiopia) under the Christian ruler there. In 622, people from the city of Yathrib, later called Medina, to the north of Mecca, invited Muhammad to go and live there. The Prophet and his followers took up the invitation. Their migration, known as the *hijrah*, forms the start of the Islamic era. Eventually Muhammad defeated the pagans and cleared the idols from the Ka'ba, so Islam could flourish in Mecca, too.

Muhammad's face is veiled because Islam does not allow him to be depicted.

The archangel Gabriel

The Buraq

THE NIGHT JOURNEY

One night the archangel Gabriel woke Muhammad and led him to a steed called the *Buraq*, which the Prophet mounted (p. 61). The Buraq carried Muhammad to the "Furthest Mosque" in Jerusalem, from where he ascended to heaven.

MUHAMMAD'S TOMB

The Prophet died in the lap of his favorite wife, 'A'isha, in her apartment near the mosque at Medina. His tomb was built where he died. Later, his close Companions Abu Bakr and 'Umar, the first two caliphs, were buried on either side.

Pattern based on names of the Companions

COMPANIONS

The Prophet's Companions were his closest followers. They listened carefully to his teachings, memorized the Qur'an, and passed it on to others before it was written down.

9

The Qur'an

IN THE YEAR 610, the archangel Gabriel appeared to the Prophet Muhammad and through Gabriel, Allah began to reveal the Qur'an, the holy book of Islam. This continued for 22 years. Muslims believe that the Qur'an, Allah's final revelation to humanity, completes the sacred writings of the Jews and Christians, but is on a higher level because its text consists of Allah's actual words. Ever since the Qur'an was revealed, Muslims have preserved its words, first learning them by heart, and later also writing them down. They aim to live by the Qur'an.

QUR'AN CONTAINER
This beautiful inlaid box is designed to contain a copy of the Qur'an divided into 30 sections. One section is read on each night of Ramadan, the month of fasting, a time when the Qur'an is read intensively.

Bold *Kufic* script

KUFIC SCRIPT
Arabic can be written using several different types of script, the earliest of which is called Kufic, from the town of Kufah (in modern Iraq). This example of eastern Kufic is from a copy of the Qur'an written out before the year 1000. The script has an angular but elegant appearance with long upright and horizontal strokes.

Eastern *Kufic* script

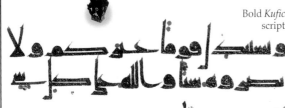

DECORATED QUR'AN
This copy of the Qur'an is open at the beginning of one of its 114 chapters, or *suras*. Each *sura* has a name that comes from a notable word that occurs in its text.

This box gives the number of verses in the sura. The box at the top gives the name of the sura.

"Praise belongs to Allah, the Lord of the worlds, the Merciful, the Compassionate, the Master of the Day of Judgment. Thee only do we serve; to Thee alone we pray for help. Guide us on the straight path, the path of those whom Thou has blessed, not of those against whom Thou are wrathful, nor of those who are astray."

SURA AL-FATIHA, **OPENING CHAPTER, THE QUR'AN**

The text on this page is the opening chapter, Sura al-Fatiha, *which is translated below to the left.*

ON A GEMSTONE

In the eyes of a Muslim, this gemstone (below) has been made far more valuable as it has a Qur'anic inscription on it, which is translated below.

"Allah – there is no god but He, the Living, the Everlasting. Slumber seizes Him not, neither sleep; to Him belongs all that is in the Heavens and the Earth..."

AYAT AL-KURSI, THRONE VERSE, THE QUR'AN

TILE AND TEXT

All over the Muslim world, beautifully written quotations from the Qur'an are used for artistic decoration. Muslims everywhere learn Arabic, the language of the Qur'an. This shared knowledge brings together Muslims from all countries and backgrounds.

MUSHAF

When people talk about "the Qur'an," they are usually referring to a book that has the Qur'an written in it. However, originally the Qur'an was recited only and Muslims learned it by heart. Later, it was written down and the written version was called a *mushaf*, which means a collection of pages. A *mushaf* will usually indicate whether each *sura* was revealed at Mecca or Medina.

WRITING IT DOWN

Copying the text of the Qur'an is something that must be done with care and reverence – none of Allah's words must be altered. To make a handwritten copy of the Qur'an like this is an activity of great religious devotion.

The Five Pillars of Islam

"In the name of Allah, the Merciful, the Compassionate."

CRESCENT MOON AND STAR
A crescent moon with a star above it was used as a symbol by the Turks in the 15th century. Since then it has become the symbol of Islam. The words of the *Shahada* in Arabic calligraphy have been used here to form the shape of the moon. The words, "In the name of Allah, the Merciful, the Compassionate," make the star.

SHAHADA
The Muslim profession of faith is called the *Shahada*. The English translation of it is: "There is no god but God; Muhammad is the messenger of God." Muslims use the Arabic word for God, which is "Allah." When Muslims use the term Allah, they are referring to the same God that is worshipped by Christians and Jews. The words of the *Shahada* are heard often in the Muslim world because they are repeated during the call to prayer. The *Shahada* is normally whispered in a Muslim baby's ear at birth and at the time of death.

THERE ARE FIVE FUNDAMENTAL requirements of Islam, called the Five Pillars of Islam. The first and most important is the profession of faith. Islam, which means "submission" and comes from the word "peace," is considered by Muslims to be a restating of the same truth – belief in the one God – that was revealed to the Christians and the Jews. This faith was revealed through all God's prophets, including Moses and Jesus, or Musa and 'Isa as they are known in Arabic. Muslims believe that God's final and most universal message was revealed to the last of the prophets – the Prophet Muhammad. Faith in this one God is the basic belief of the Islamic religion. The remaining four Pillars of Islam require all Muslims to be committed to prayer, almsgiving, fasting, and the pilgrimage to Mecca.

Prayer

Muslims must pray at five set times during the day. These regular prayers, known as *salah*, make up the second Pillar of Islam. Muslims may pray on their own or in a group, but every Friday at midday, Muslim men are required to gather together for *salat al-juma'a*, or Friday prayers. Friday prayers are led by an imam (literally "one who stands in front"), who will also give a sermon, or *khutba*.

All members of the community are considered equal in the eyes of Allah so they all perform the same rituals of ablution and prayer.

RISE UP FOR PRAYER
Five times each day the *adhan*, or call to prayer, is heard in Muslim communities. The times for prayer are between first light and sunrise (*fajr*), just after noon (*zuhr*), in late afternoon (*'asr*), after sunset (*maghrib*), and evening (*'isha*). The traditional practice is for someone to make the call from the minaret. The first muezzin was Bilal, a freed black slave, chosen for his fine voice.

PREPARING FOR PRAYER
Before prayer, a Muslim must prepare by ridding the mind of distracting thoughts and by cleansing the body. Ritual washing is normally done using running water – either at the fountain at the mosque or using a tap and basin in the home. In places where there is no water, such as the desert, Muslims may use sand or a stone for ritual cleansing.

IN THE DIRECTION OF MECCA

Because Muslims face the Ka'ba in Mecca during prayers, they need to know the direction, *qibla*, of the city. In the Middle Ages, people made instruments to determine the direction. In mosques, a niche, *mihrab*, in the wall indicates the direction of Mecca.

Qibla indicator

PRAYER BEADS

Allah is referred to in many different ways, known as *al-asma al-husna*, meaning the 99 beautiful names. Many Muslim names, such as 'Abd al-Rahman, servant of the Merciful One, are based on one of these names. The string of 99 beads, like a rosary, that a Muslim uses in private prayer, is a reminder of the 99 Divine names.

PRAYER MAT

The majority of Muslims pray on a mat, and some people take this with them wherever they go, so that they are always able to use it. Prayer rugs are often beautifully made, but any mat, from a silk rug to a piece of reed matting, may be used, it is also permissible to pray on the uncovered ground, provided that it is clean.

Prayer beads may be used to repeat the 99 beautiful names, or to repeat other phrases used in prayer.

Iranian prayer mat

1 THE RAK'A BEGINS
The words Allahu Akbar – Allah is greater (than all else) – open the *rak'a*. Then Allah is praised, and the first *sura*, or chapter, of the Qur'an, called *al-Fatiha* – the Opening – is spoken, together with a second *sura*.

5 PEACE
The final stage is called *salam*, or peace. The person looks to left and right, and then says, "Peace be with you and the mercy of Allah." These words are addressed to all present, seen and unseen.

4 SITTING
This seated position, called *julus*, gives the opportunity for a short silent prayer. Then the prostration is repeated. The sequence concludes with a short prayer for the community of Muslims and for the worshipper's sins to be forgiven.

3 PROSTRATION
This position, known as *sujud*, shows the Muslim's humility. The worshipper says silently, "Glory to my Lord the Most High. Allah is greater."

2 BOWING DOWN
When another passage from the Qur'an has been recited, the worshipper bows down, to show respect for Allah. This motion, called *ruku'*, is followed by *qiyam*, standing and praising Allah.

Stages of prayer

Prayer is performed following a precise order of words and motions. Each unit of this order is called a *rak'a* and is composed of several stages. During prayers the *rak'a* is repeated two, three, or four times – the exact number depends on which of the five daily prayers is being performed.

Continued on next page

Almsgiving

The giving of alms (gifts) to the poor and needy is very important in Islam. Of all the ways in which one can give to the poor, the most formal is by paying a tax called *zakat*, which is one of the Five Pillars of Islam. The amount of *zakat* that a person has to pay is worked out as a percentage of their wealth. The tax is distributed among the poor and may also be used to help other needy members of society.

WATER SUPPLY
In addition to paying *zakat*, a person may make other personal donations to help the community. These can provide useful facilities such as this public drinking fountain in Istanbul, Turkey. Many Muslim countries are in dry areas where water can be hard to come by, so giving money for a fountain is especially useful.

PUBLIC BATHS
Hygiene is very important in Islam, and baths are a common sight in towns in Muslim countries. They are often paid for by donations. A typical public bath has a changing room, often roofed with a shallow dome, connected to a series of rooms at different temperatures. The hottest of all is the steam room, where the bather works up a sweat before being cleaned and massaged.

HOSPITALS
The places where the sick are treated are another group of facilities that have been paid for by almsgiving. This beautiful latticed window is part of a hospital originally financed with almsgiving contributions. Medicine was one area where the Muslim world made many advances before the West (p. 30).

MONEY OR GOODS
Zakat is commonly paid in money but may also be given in the form of goods. In both cases, rates of payment are laid down, starting at 2.5 percent of a person's wealth. A person's home and other essential items are not counted when determining what they will pay. The word *zakat* means "purification", because it is believed that giving up part of your wealth purifies what remains.

FOOD FOR THE POOR
In some parts of Muslim India, large cooking pots, or *deghs*, are used to prepare food outdoors. At the shrine of Ajmer, two *deghs* are used to make food for the needy, and people visiting the shrine make charitable gifts of food for the pots.

FOR LASTING GOOD
This document details a gift made to the state for good works. This type of gift is known as a *waqf*, and once given, it cannot be reclaimed. Gifts like this go toward the upkeep of mosques and buildings such as hospitals.

A PROPER MEAL
During Ramadan, Muslims break their fast after sunset with a light snack, which may consist simply of a few dates with water. Sunset prayers are followed by the main meal. This is a bigger meal, but should not be too large because Muslims are not encouraged to eat heavily after the day's fast. In addition, the snack should have already taken the edge off a person's hunger, so a simple dish, such as vegetable soup with bread, may be eaten.

JOYFUL PROCESSION
When the great solemnity of the month of Ramadan comes to an end, there may be a procession. This illustration, from a 13th-century book from Baghdad, shows a procession accompanied with trumpets and banners.

Fasting

Muhammad received the first revelation of the Qur'an during the month of Ramadan, and this month has a special significance in Islam. Every day during Ramadan, Muslims fast from dawn to sunset, avoiding food, drink, and sexual relations. Although this fast, or *sawm*, is one of the Pillars of Islam, not everyone has to go without food. For example, those who are too sick to fast, women who are pregnant, and very young children may be excused.

SIGNALING RAMADAN
In many Muslim countries, it is the custom to fire cannons before the first day of Ramadan, to signal the beginning of the month. Cannons are also used to signal the beginning and end of each day of Ramadan.

ENDING RAMADAN
The end of Ramadan is marked by the festival of *'Id al-Fitr* – the feast of the breaking of the fast – (p. 60). At the beginning of this festival, the whole community gathers at an outdoor prayer area (or at a mosque) to perform the *'Id* prayer. Celebrations last for three days, during which time alms are given to the poor and friends may exchange gifts.

Continued on next page

Pilgrimage

The final Pillar of Islam is pilgrimage, or *hajj*. All Muslims aim to perform this "greater pilgrimage" once in their lives. *Hajj* involves a series of rites that take place annually over several days at the Sacred Mosque at Mecca and the nearby areas of Mina, Muzdalifa, and Arafat. A shorter pilgrimage to Mecca, known as *'umrah*, forms part of the *hajj*, but may be performed by itself at any time of the year.

CLOTHS OF THE KA'BA

The Ka'ba (below) is a stone building, roughly 43 ft (13 m) across, that stands at the center of the Sacred Mosque at Mecca. It is a sanctuary dedicated to God that dates back to the time of Adam. The Ka'ba is covered with a black cloth embroidered with verses of the Qur'an. Every year, the cloth is renewed, and pieces of the old cloth (left) are given away. These fragments are treated with reverence, as is this cloth that once hung inside the Ka'ba.

Piece of cloth from the Ka'ba

AT THE KA'BA

Upon arrival in Mecca, the pilgrims perform *'umrah*, when they circle seven times around the Ka'ba and then pray near the Station of Abraham. In memory of Hagar, the mother of Abraham's eldest son, Ishmael, the pilgrims then run back and forth between two small hills known as Safa and Marwa after drinking water from the well of Zamzam.

HAJJ

After performing *'umrah*, the pilgrims leave Mecca and travel to the valley of Mina. On the second day, they go to Arafat and pray for forgiveness. This is said to give pilgrims a foretaste of the Day of Judgment, when they will rise from the dead, have their souls judged by Allah, and enter paradise if they are worthy. On their way back, they stop at Muzdalifa, where they spend part of the night resting, praying, and gathering small pebbles before returning to Mina. On the third day, they throw seven of the pebbles at the largest of the three stone pillars, which represents the temptations of Satan. For the following two days, the pilgrims stay at Mina and throw further pebbles at the pillars. They must also make an animal sacrifice. They then wash, and clip their hair or shave their heads, to symbolize a new beginning, before returning to Mecca to make the final seven circuits around the Ka'ba.

together with a hanging lamp.

GUIDEBOOK

An ancient guidebook to Mecca illustrates features of the Sacred Mosque. It shows the stepped *minbar*, from which the sermon is preached (p. 19), together with a hanging lamp.

Quotation from the Qur'an saying that the pilgrimage to Mecca is a duty for all who can make their way there

Tile with the Plan of the Sacred Mosque at Mecca, known in Arabic as the Masjid al-Haram

Rows of arches surrounding the Ka'ba were hung with oil lights. Today the Mosque is lit electrically.

The Ka'ba

The multazam – an area of wall thought to be particularly holy

The Station of Abraham, from which Abraham directed the rebuilding of the Ka'ba

The minbar

The Black Stone

PLACE OF ABRAHAM
The Ka'ba is said to have been founded by Adam, the father of humankind, who is considered by Muslims to be the first prophet. It was rebuilt by Abraham and his son, Ishmael. Set into one corner of the Ka'ba is the Black Stone, a meteorite, said to have been used by Adam when the Ka'ba was first built. The Black Stone was lost, and then found again by Abraham and put in its present position.

PILGRIM'S HOUSE
In some places it is traditional for pilgrims to commemorate their journey by decorating the walls of their houses when they return home. The paintings on this Egyptian house show the airplane on which the pilgrim flew to Saudi Arabia, the Ka'ba, and the Grand Mosque at Mecca, and the pilgrim himself, wearing the costume of *ihram*.

IHRAM
Pilgrims must be in a special state of consecration, or holiness, achieved by washing and declaring their intention. Male pilgrims wear a simple costume that symbolizes *ihram*. It consists of two large pieces of seamless, unstitched, white cloth.

THE ROAD TO MECCA
This 13th-century picture shows the colorful tents of a group of rich pilgrims. They are on their way to Mecca and have not yet put on the costume of *ihram*. Pilgrims still use tents today. At the time of *hajj*, the area around Mina is filled with thousands of pure white tents. Pilgrims will usually also visit the Prophet's Mosque in Medina during their stay.

The mosque

CENTERS OF LEARNING
Many big mosques have libraries, which contain books on religious subjects, including Islamic law. In addition, it is common for mosques to have schools where children learn to memorize and recite the Qur'an.

MOSQUES ARE BUILDINGS that are specifically used for prayer and are open for prayer all the way through the week. In addition, mosques fulfill several other functions in the Muslim community. They provide places where religious discussions can take place, and where education and charitable work can be organized. Most mosques serve their local area and form the spiritual center of the community. They are built and run by local people, though they may be funded by donations from the wealthy. In addition, a town has one main mosque, where Friday prayers are held.

INSIDE A MOSQUE
Mosques vary enormously in design, from simple plain rooms to vast ornate buildings – there is no one standard design. All that is really needed is a space in which the community can pray and some way of indicating the direction of Mecca. But there are standards of behavior and dress that must be observed inside every mosque. People take off their shoes and cover their heads before going in, and often an area of the mosque is reserved for women.

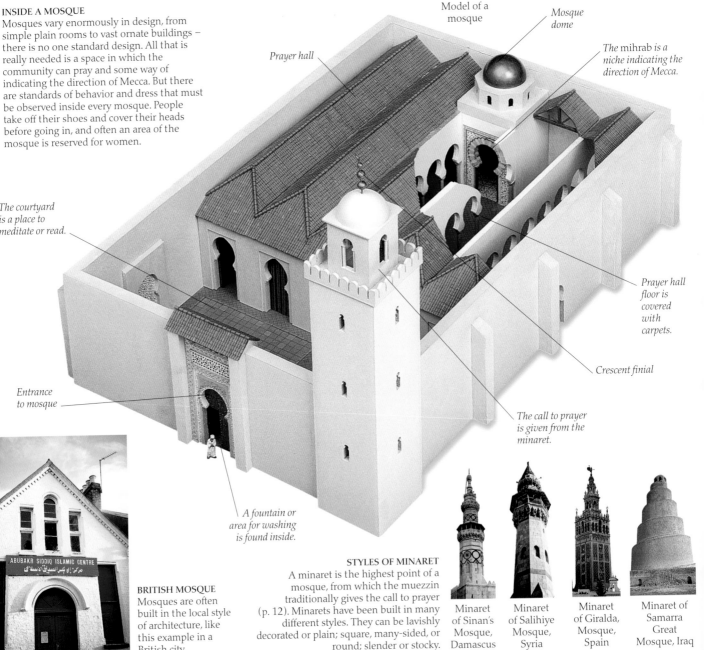

Prayer hall

Model of a mosque

Mosque dome

The mihrab is a niche indicating the direction of Mecca.

The courtyard is a place to meditate or read.

Prayer hall floor is covered with carpets.

Crescent finial

Entrance to mosque

The call to prayer is given from the minaret.

A fountain or area for washing is found inside.

ABUBAKR SIDDIQ ISLAMIC CENTRE

BRITISH MOSQUE
Mosques are often built in the local style of architecture, like this example in a British city.

STYLES OF MINARET
A minaret is the highest point of a mosque, from which the muezzin traditionally gives the call to prayer (p. 12). Minarets have been built in many different styles. They can be lavishly decorated or plain; square, many-sided, or round; slender or stocky.

Minaret of Sinan's Mosque, Damascus

Minaret of Salihiye Mosque, Syria

Minaret of Giralda, Mosque, Spain

Minaret of Samarra Great Mosque, Iraq

MINBAR

At Friday prayers the congregation listens to the *khutba*, a sermon given by the imam from a raised pulpit called the *minbar*. Some *minbars*, which can be beautifully adorned with inlay and carving, have survived from 1,000 years ago.

OIL LAMP

The traditional way of lighting a mosque was to use oil lamps. These large, hanging lamps could be brightly decorated, like this example of bronze covered with gold and silver, so that they reflected the light and shone more brightly. People who wanted to give alms often made gifts of money for oil for the lamps in their mosque.

15th-century mosque lamp

Mosque finial of Selimiye Mosque in Turkey

Elaborate tile decoration

BLUE MOSQUE IN ISTANBUL

In 1453, the Ottomans took over Constantinople (modern Istanbul). The Christian churches there were lavishly decorated and roofed with domes. Ottoman architects built their mosques in a similar style. One of the greatest is the Sultan Ahmed Mosque, known as the Blue Mosque because of its blue-tiled interior.

SYDNEY MOSQUE

The first Muslims to reach Australia were Afghan and Punjabi camel drivers, arriving between 1867 and 1918 to provide essential outback transportation services. Many more Muslims arrived during the late 20th century.

AFRICAN MOSQUE

The earliest mosques had more simple designs, like this 16th-century mosque in Africa. Domes and intricate decoration developed later. The nature of the building, however, is not significant in a mosque. Its function as a meeting place to pray is the most important thing.

MOSQUE DECORATION

As Muslims prospered, they devoted more of their wealth to their faith, and some mosques were adorned with sumptuous decoration, like these tiles atop a minaret in Turkey. Carpets for the prayer hall were another favorite gift.

The caliphate

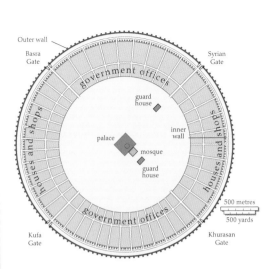

Outer wall
Basra Gate
Syrian Gate
government offices
guard house
inner wall
palace
mosque
guard house
houses and shops
houses and shops
government offices
Kufa Gate
Khurasan Gate
500 metres
500 yards

THE ROUND CITY OF BAGHDAD
The first dynasty of Islam was the Umayyad, who ruled from Damascus, Syria. In 749, they were replaced by the Abbasid caliphs who ruled for over 500 years from their capital in Baghdad, Iraq. The city was founded in 763 and was planned as a great circle. This shape, with gates aligned with the compass points, was like a map of the universe.

IN 632, THE PROHET MUHAMMAD died leaving no obvious successor, so prominent Muslims came together to choose a leader. They elected Abu Bakr and gave him the title *khalifa* (caliph), which means "successor" or "viceroy." Some people thought that the right candidate was 'Ali, the Prophet's cousin, who had married Fatima, the Prophet's daughter. Those who favored 'Ali as caliph became known as Shi'i Muslims, "supporters" of 'Ali. In 656, 'Ali became caliph, but Muslims were still divided about how the caliph should be chosen. Sunni Muslims supported the system of an elected caliphate. Shi'i Muslims believed that the caliphs should be descended from 'Ali and Fatima.

THE ROLE OF THE CALIPH
The caliph was the symbolic head of the Muslim community throughout the world. He was expected to rule in accordance with Islamic principles and to lead the army. He also gave authority to Muslim leaders who were often very powerful in their own right. The Mamluk sultanate, for example, ruled in Egypt until the 16th century. This is a Mamluk mosque lamp. Such lamps were often decorated with script from the *Sura al-Nur* of the Qur'an (right).

"Allah is the Light of the Heavens and the Earth; the likeness of His Light is as a niche wherein is a lamp."

SURA AL-NUR, LIGHT CHAPTER, THE QUR'AN

THE FIRST FOUR CALIPHS
Abu Bakr, 'Umar, 'Uthman, and 'Ali were the first four caliphs and are greatly revered. As close Companions of the Prophet, they followed his example. Because of this they are known as the Rightly Guided Caliphs.

EARLY CALIPH
Representation of living creatures is discouraged in Islam because it is believed that Allah alone should have the divine right of creation. However, this early portrait shows a caliph, in a style imitated from pre-Islamic Persian coins.

Dhu'l-Faqar, the twin-bladed sword of 'Ali

CALIPH'S GIFT
Rulers like eighth-century caliph Harun al-Rashid were very powerful. Harun exchanged gifts with Charlemagne, the Frankish emperor who ruled a vast area of Western Europe. He sent Charlemagne this jeweled pitcher, with an elephant.

Repeating calligraphic inscription

TIRAZ
Some caliphs gave courtiers, ambassadors, and foreign rulers lengths of specially made cloth – *tiraz* – or robes, woven with calligraphy. In particular, this was a custom of the Shi'i Fatimid caliphs (who claimed to be descendents of 'Ali and Fatima) of Cairo. The cloths were inscribed with the caliphs' names, Islamic prayers, or poems, and were highly prized.

Calligraphy reads, "Allah, Muhammad, Fatima, and 'Ali, Hasan and Husayn."

SHI'I STANDARD
In 680 at Kerbala, the army of the Umayyad caliph killed Hussayn, son of 'Ali and Fatima. The battle standard (above) was used to mark the point at which the Shi'i army collected before the battle began and was then a focal point for the army. What happened at Kerbala divided Shi'i and Sunni Muslims still more deeply. Today, around one-tenth of all Muslims are Shi'i.

LADEN WITH GIFTS
One of the duties of the caliph was to protect the holy cities of Mecca and Medina, together with pilgrims journeying there. Pilgrims often traveled with camels heavily loaded with gifts.

Inscription proclaiming the unity of Allah

UMAYYAD COIN
Abd al-Malik, one of the Umayyad caliphs, minted this coin when they ruled from Damascus, Syria. After their defeat by the Abbasids, an offshoot of the Umayyad caliphate ruled Muslim lands in the West from Spain.

ATATURK
The last caliphs were the Ottoman rulers of Turkey. In 1923, Turkey's first president, Kemal Atatürk, came to power. He decided to modernize his country and in 1924 he abolished the caliphate.

First conquests

THE FIRST THREE CALIPHS Abu Bakr, 'Umar, and 'Uthman, expanded their territory quickly, creating an empire that eventually stretched from the Arabian Peninsula to Spain. Much land was gained by military conquest, but Islam also spread peacefully into areas where local rulers made alliances with the caliphs. People of other religions living in these areas – Jews, Christians, and Zoroastrians – became known as *dhimmis* (protected people) because they were protected in return for the payment of a tax. Later, other peoples, including Hindus in western India, also became *dhimmis*.

EXPANDING EMPIRE
By the end of 'Uthman's reign in 656, the empire included Arabia, Palestine, Syria, Egypt, Libya, Iraq, large parts of Persia (modern-day Iran), and Sind (modern-day Pakistan). The Umayyad dynasty (661–750) expanded into the rest of North Africa and Spain and pushed eastward.

CROWN OF RECCESUINTH
This crown was worn by an early Muslim ruler of Spain, at the request of his wife, who was a princess of the Germanic people, the Visigoths.

MAP OF JERUSALEM
This mosaic map shows Jerusalem in the sixth century. It must have looked like this in 638 when, during the reign of caliph 'Umar, the Muslims conquered the city. For many centuries, the city's Islamic rulers governed Jerusalem in a way that was tolerant of the Jews and Christians who lived there and regarded it as a holy place.

ROCK OF GIBRALTAR
Muslim forces landed in Spain in 711, arriving first on the Rock of Gibraltar under their commander, a Berber former slave, Tariq, from whom Gibraltar takes its name (Jebel Tariq). By 715, they had taken over most of Spain, settling mainly in the south, and soon their armies were entering France.

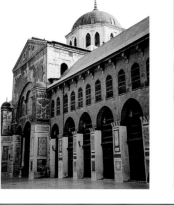

MOSQUE AT DAMASCUS
Under the Umayyad dynasty, the city of Damascus in Syria became the capital of the Islamic empire. The Umayyads built the Great Mosque in the early eighth century.

MOSQUE DECORATION
Mosques were built all around the empire, and many were lavishly decorated. This arch, above a doorway at the Great Mosque in Damascus, shows how Muslim stone masons used different marbles, together with inlays and mosaics made of other brightly colored stones.

RUINS OF CARTHAGE

Roman triumphal arch, Carthage

The great North African city of Carthage, first the home of the Phoenicians, had been ruled by the Romans before it became an outpost of the Christian Byzantine empire for a short time. The victim of many battles, in 697–8 Carthage fell to Muslim armies. The native Berber population who lived there soon accepted Islam and joined the westward drive of the Muslim forces.

CHARLES MARTEL, KING OF THE FRANKS

In the eighth century, much of Western Europe was ruled by a Germanic people called the Franks, under their king, Charles Martel. In 732, Charles defeated the Muslim army between Tours and Poitiers, France, which marked the northwestern limit of the Muslim empire. Five years later, he also drove the Muslims out of southern France.

OUT IN FORCE

This image from an early manuscript shows Muslim soldiers gathering near their tents. Soldiers like these, efficient and well disciplined, were greatly feared in Western Europe. They advanced as far as France to conquer areas such as Languedoc and Burgundy.

BATTLE STANDARD

In 1212, Spain saw a battle at Navas de Tolosa, between the Almohads, the local Muslim dynasty, and a Christian army. The Almohads, who marched behind this standard, were defeated, and Muslim power in Spain was weakened.

Scholars and teachers

AL-AZHAR UNIVERSITY
Cairo's al-Azhar University was founded in the 10th century and became the world's most famous Islamic university. Renowned for its philosophical and theological scholarship, its name means "the resplendent." Many academic traditions, such as the distinction between graduates and undergraduates, began at al-Azhar.

LEARNING HAS ALWAYS PLAYED a huge part in the Islamic world. A system of education developed in which children learned to memorize and recite the text of the Qur'an at school. When they had mastered this, they could become students at a higher-level school called a *madrasah*. Still more advanced study could be followed at university level. Muslim education has always had a religious basis, and the high standards produced scholars in a range of fields, from mathematics to poetry.

AVICENNA
The scholar Ibn Sina (980–1037), known in the West as Avicenna, wrote many important books on medicine and philosophy. In both fields, he developed the work of the ancient Greeks.

MADRASAH AT CAIRO
A *madrasah* was a school in which subjects such as law, logic, mathematics, and history were taught. *Madrasahs* were usually arranged around a courtyard, with large halls for teaching and smaller rooms for the students.

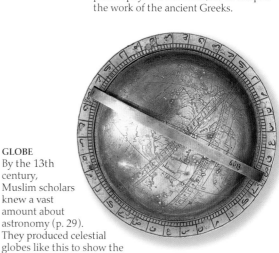

GLOBE
By the 13th century, Muslim scholars knew a vast amount about astronomy (p. 29). They produced celestial globes like this to show the positions of stars in the sky.

SCHOLAR'S TOMB
Sometimes a famous scholar is commemorated with a large tomb. Bin Ali, a notable scholar of the 14th century from Yemen, was buried in this striking double-domed tomb near Dhofar, Oman.

LIBRARY BOOKS
Centers of learning grew up in big cities such as Baghdad, Iraq, and Damascus, Syria, and these had libraries that were often much larger than the collections in Western cities and universities.

QUR'AN
Arabic scholarship has always been central to Islam. Muslims traditionally learn to recite the entire Qur'an by heart, and they always recite it in the original Arabic, no matter what language they use in everyday life.

LAW BOOK
Muslim scholars produced some very advanced laws. From the earliest times, for example, Muslim women – unlike women in the West – had the right to own and inherit property. This book contains information about how inheritance was calculated.

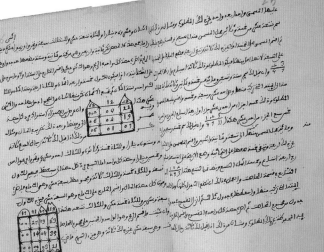

A MULLAH
A mullah is a person who is learned in religion. Most mullahs have had a formal religious training, but the title can be given to someone with a reputation for religious scholarship.

POETRY READING
Recited or set to music, poetry was important in Arabia even before the time of Muhammad. It continued to be popular. In addition to religious subjects, common poetic themes were love and politics.

Inkpot made of gold and agate

AGATE INKPOT
Calligraphy was an important and respected art. While most writing materials were simple, some very fine pieces, like this 19th century inkpot, were also made.

Continued on next page

Writing

For Muslims, writing is one of the most important of all skills. Because Muslims believe that the Qur'an contains the words of Allah, scribes wish to reproduce those words correctly and with as much beauty as possible. Many Muslims therefore practice calligraphy, the art of beautiful writing. Calligraphy does not only appear in books. It is also used to adorn buildings and other objects, providing decoration that carries a meaning.

EARLY SCHOLARS
This illustration from a 16th-century Persian text shows two children at Qur'anic school. Here they would receive the traditional education of young Muslims, learning to read, write, and recite the text of the Qur'an by heart.

Flowing maghribi *script is one popular style of Islamic calligraphy.*

STUDENTS AT WORK
Some Muslim children, like these in Uzbekistan, still attend traditional Qur'anic schools. In many places, modern schooling has replaced this as the main type of education, though children may attend both kinds of school.

HORSE CALLIGRAPHY
Some Muslim calligraphers can make beautiful pictures using the curving forms of Arabic script. This horse is made up entirely of Arabic script, adorned with different colored inks.

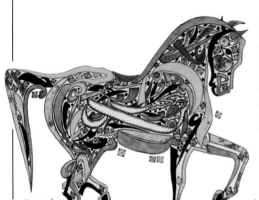

Inscription written in legible form

STONE BANNERS
Calligraphy is used on many Islamic buildings. At this *madrasah* in Konya, Turkey, bands of carved calligraphy curve around the doorway and cross in a knot-like form above it, like fabric banners.

PEN AND INK
Early calligraphers used pens made out of pieces of reed (left), cut to a point with a sharp knife. Black ink was made from soot, mixed with a little water to make it flow.

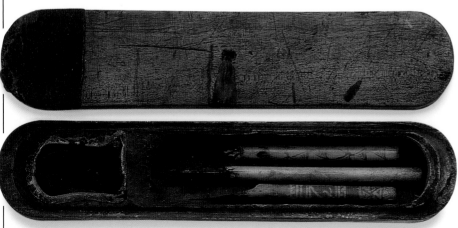

Animal-hair calligraphy brushes for larger characters

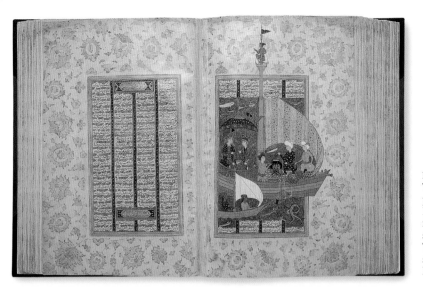

INKWELL
Two bands of calligraphy decorate this inkwell, which was made in Iran in the 16th century. It would have inspired its user to produce writing of beauty and elegance.

BOOK OF KINGS
This book is an epic poem composed in Iran. It is written in a flowing form of Arabic script called *nasta'liq*. The long curves in the script are said to look like birds' wings.

BOOKBINDER
An Indian craftsman holds the pages of a book together to bind them. Bookbinding became an important craft because of the need to protect copies of the Qur'an.

Animal-hair calligraphy brushes for smaller characters

BROAD-BRUSH EFFECTS
Although a lot of calligraphy is done with pen and ink, an animal-hair brush is another useful tool for broad strokes and for filling in colors between black outlines. These brushes are made with goat and wolf hair.

ARABIAN NIGHTS
The Thousand and One Nights, or *Arabian Nights*, is a collection of stories said to have been told to a king, Shahryar, by his wife Shahrazad. Full of adventure, these magical stories are still entertaining readers today.

The spread of learning

ISLAMIC SCHOLARSHIP IS NOT just based on the study of the Qur'an. In a famous saying, Muslim scholars are told to "Seek knowledge, even unto China." In the Middle Ages, there were well-known Muslim scholars in many fields, from astronomy and mathematics to medicine and natural science, and in most areas their ideas were among the most advanced in the world. The Islamic scholars gained much of their knowledge from the ancient world. They translated the works of ancient Greek scholars, preserving information that had been lost or forgotten. The Muslim scholars then built on this with their own original work, carefully recording all their discoveries.

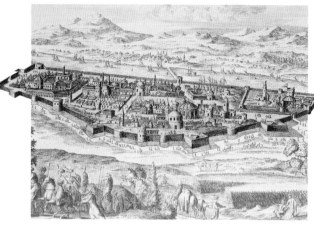

BAGHDAD
Under the Abbasids, the walled city of Baghdad became an important center of learning, with its own university and numerous schools. The city was at its height during the reign of Caliph Harun al-Rashid, who ruled from 786–809. At this time, it was the intellectual center of the Muslim world.

Horseshoe Arch, Cordoba, Andalusia, Spain

Al-Idrisi map showing what was thought to be the shape of the known world in the 12th century

Africa

ARCHITECTURAL STYLE
Wherever Islamic people have settled for any length of time, they have built using the distinctive Islamic architectural style. These buildings often had simple exteriors which concealed lavish interiors decorated with geometric patterns and calligraphy. The horseshoe arch was also popular because it was elegant and withstood stress and strain well.

Arabia

Asia

Unlike modern western maps, south is at the top and north is at the bottom.

AL-IDRISI
Writer and traveler al-Idrisi (1099–1180) was born in Ceuta, Morocco, but worked for much of his life for the Norman king, Roger II of Sicily. He drew this map of the known world for King Roger and also wrote a book on geography, describing the world north of the equator.

Europe

Shaft turned by donkey to operate scoop

Scoop raises water into system of channels through fields

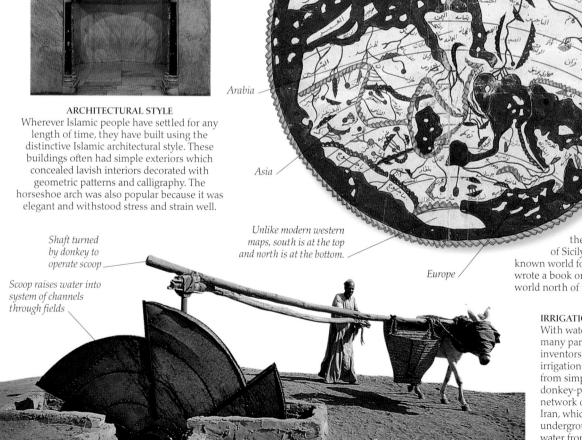

IRRIGATION TECHNIQUES
With water in short supply in many parts of the Islamic world, inventors used their skill to build irrigation devices. These ranged from simple systems, such as this donkey-powered water scoop, to a network of irrigation channels in Iran, which were built underground to reduce loss of water from evaporation. These channels are called *qanat*, and some are 12 miles (19 km) long.

Astronomy

The science of astronomy was important to Muslims because it could be used to figure out the direction of Mecca, so that people knew which way to face during prayers. It also helped them to determine the correct times to pray. As a result, Islamic astronomy became highly advanced. Astronomers developed better instruments, made precise tables showing the movements of the planets, and put together accurate calendars. We are still influenced by these scientists – the names of certain stars derive from Arabic words.

JAIPUR OBSERVATORY
This observatory at Jaipur, India, was built during the 18th century. Many of its instruments are built of stone. These include great curving quadrants, which astronomers used to measure the height of planets as they moved across the sky. The astronomers at Jaipur were successful because they drew on knowledge from both the Arab world and from earlier Indian scientists.

ISTANBUL OBSERVATORY
In 1575, when the Ottoman empire was at its height, the astronomer Taqi ad-Din founded an observatory at Galata (now part of Istanbul, Turkey). This painting of the time shows the astronomers with their equipment, which includes a globe, a sand glass for timing, items for drawing, and all kinds of sighting devices.

Persian astrolabe

Scales showing the positions of different stars

ASTROLABE
The astrolabe is an instrument for measuring the height of a star or planet in the sky. It was probably invented by the ancient Greeks, but Muslim scholars and craft workers developed the instrument, making it more accurate and incorporating more data to show the positions of a variety of different stars. It was especially useful to travelers because it could help them to determine their position at sea.

Central pivot

Rotating arm with pointer

Written instructions for using quadrant

Plumb line

Scale

Arabic quadrant

QUADRANT
This was the simplest instrument for measuring the height of a star. It consisted of a quarter-circle-shaped framework with a scale on the curving part of the frame and a plumb line hanging down vertically. The user looked at a star through a hole in the frame. The height of the star was shown at the point where the plumb line touched the scale.

ASTRONOMY LESSON
This group of scholars is watching as their teacher demonstrates an astrolabe. There were many observatories where lessons like this would have been held. These centers expanded rapidly in the ninth century, during the reign of Caliph 'Abd Allah al-Ma'mun. The caliph founded the House of Wisdom in Baghdad, which included an observatory, and ordered the scientists there to produce more accurate astronomical tables.

Continued on next page

Title page of
the *Canon of
Medicine*

Medicine

Early Islamic medicine was very
sophisticated for its time.
Doctors knew a great deal about
the diagnosis and treatment of
diseases, anatomy, childcare,
public health, and even
psychiatry – and much of this
knowledge is still relevant
today. Medicine was also well
taught, with students
traveling thousands of
miles to study at famous
centers such as Baghdad's
'Adudi hospital.

CANON OF MEDICINE
The most famous book by scholar Ibn Sina (p. 24)
is the *Canon of Medicine*. Ibn Sina based much of
this book on the writings of ancient Greek
physicians. A huge work, it covers such basic
subjects as anatomy and hygiene, describes a vast
range of diseases and injuries, and lists hundreds
of different medicines.

THE ART OF THE PHARMACIST
The Islamic world produced the first skilled,
specially trained pharmacists, who made their
own medicines and worked closely with
physicians. By the early ninth century, privately
owned pharmacies were opening in Baghdad,
where a flourishing trade with Asia and Africa
provided a variety of medicinal herbs and spices.
Pharmacies were soon appearing in other cities.

*Ivory handle
decorated with
a lion head motif*

*Metal handle
decorated with
a ram's head*

Eighteenth-century surgical knives

UNDER THE KNIFE
The great 10th-century surgeon az-Zahrawi, from Islamic
Spain, wrote a book describing techniques such as
treating wounds, setting bones, and removing
arrows. Not all these operations were painful
because Muslim surgeons were the first to use
painkillers. Az-Zahrawi designed many types of surgical
instruments and similar ones were used for hundreds of years.

*Blade folds
into handle
for safety.*

Scalpel

Scissors

*Folding
handles*

BLOODLETTING
Like the ancient Greeks, Muslim physicians
believed that bleeding a patient could cure many
diseases. Although this practice seems crude
today, the early Islamic doctors knew a great deal
about blood and how it traveled around the body.
One 13th-century Egyptian writer, Ibn an-Nafis,
wrote about the circulation of blood, some 400
years before this was "discovered" in Europe.

HERBAL MEDICINE
The ancient Greek surgeon Dioscorides wrote a famous herbal encyclopedia that was translated into Arabic. Its five books describe all kinds of herbs, spices, roots, juices, and seeds that were used to make medicines and other preparations. This page from a 10th-century Arabic version of Dioscorides shows henna, a plant used widely in the Arab world as a dye.

IN STORAGE
Many medicines were made with fresh herbs, but these could not always be found all year round. Herbalists therefore dried leaves, seeds, and other plant parts, so that they were available for use at any time of the year. Herbs were stored in glass or pottery jars, and these were usually sealed with a cork or stopper.

Dark color to keep out light

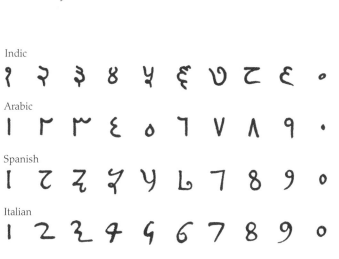

Pottery storage jars

Pointed blade for piercing and then cutting the skin

Vessel has rounded bottom to aid mixing

Mortar and pestle

WELL-PREPARED
Pharmacists and physicians often prepared medicines by grinding the ingredients together using a mortar and pestle. They made their preparations carefully, often following a standard textbook such as the 11th-century al-Aqrabadhin, which describes many different medications.

Mathematics
Modern mathematics was made possible by Islamic scholars. This was because Muslim mathematicians in Baghdad gathered ideas from both ancient Greece and India, as well as adding contributions of their own. In addition to studying subjects such as arithmetic and geometry, they also founded the science of algebra – a word that comes from the Arabic *al-jabr*, a term describing a method of solving equations.

ARABIC NUMBERS
The numbers we use today began life in India. The Indians used place-value (which gives a value to a number according to its position) and the zero, which was unknown in the West. These ideas, which made arithmetic much easier than before, were in use in India in the 6th century. They were taken up by Muslims by the 9th century and probably passed to Europe in a 12th-century translation of an Arabic book on mathematics.

Indic

Arabic

Spanish

Italian

Nomadic or settled

As ISLAM SPREAD, the faith came to people with many different lifestyles. Some were nomads, living in tents and moving from one place to another in search of new grazing lands for their animals. Others lived in settlements that varied from small oasis villages to some of the world's most sophisticated cities. Even town-dwellers were often on the move, for many were merchants, taking caravans of camels across the desert from one market to the next. In this way, both nomadic and settled people helped to spread Islam across western Asia and North Africa.

OASIS
Water trapped deep under the ground comes to the surface at oases, small patches of green among the desert's rocks and sand. People can settle here and cultivate crops such as date palms. Oases are also vital water sources for nomadic desert peoples.

ON THE THRESHOLD
In Islamic tradition, the door forms the meeting point between the private house interior and the public outside world and may have beautiful carved or painted decoration.

PERCHED ALOFT
For centuries, Yemen has been a prosperous part of Arabia. The area was ideally placed to allow the people to make money from the water-borne trade in the Red Sea and build cities with beautiful tall brick houses like these. The comings and goings in such cities made Yemen a melting pot of ideas where both main branches of Islam – Sunni and Shi'i – became well established.

TRADING PLACES
From Tangier in North Africa to Muscat in Arabia, most Muslim cities have always had markets that formed meeting places for traders all over the Islamic world. Everyone came to trade here – nomads, settled farmers and craft workers, and merchants from near and far. This coming together of peoples made markets prime places for the spread of Islam.

Wooden poles, supported by guy ropes, hold up the tent.

RIDER AND CAMEL
Camels provide ideal desert transportation because they can go for days without food or water, living off the fat in their humps. This one carries tasselled saddlebags beneath a sheepskin saddle blanket. The rider wears traditional Bedouin costume – a long white tunic covered by a sleeveless cloak with a headcloth secured by two woolen coils. These clothes protect him from both sun and wind.

*Flat, wide feet
do not sink
into the sand.*

SUPER SADDLE
Horses have always been important to the Arab people, especially those living a nomadic lifestyle. Arabian horses are still widely prized today. This saddle with matching saddle cloth is fit for the finest Arabian horse.

LIVES OF THE MONGOLS
The Mongols of Central Asia, nomads who traditionally lived in round tents called yurts or gers, conquered Islamic lands in the 13th and 14th centuries, after which many Mongols became Muslims.

BEDOUIN TENT
The Bedouins of Arabia and North Africa are desert-dwellers whose traditional life involves nomadic camel-herding. They were among the first to convert to Islam and to spread the faith. Some Bedouin still live in long, low tents, though few are now nomads.

Islamic culture

Islam quickly developed its own style, which found unique expression in each of the diverse cultures that flourished within its empire. One famous *hadith* (Islamic saying) declares, "Allah is beautiful and loves beauty." Beauty was therefore very important, and the visual arts such as architecture, calligraphy, painting, textiles, metalwork, and ceramics were encouraged. One striking feature of Islamic art is the widespread use of pattern in decoration, inspired by the love of geometry. Poetry and music were among other important forms of art.

FIT FOR A SULTAN
The Topkapi Palace in Istanbul was home to the rulers of the Ottoman empire from the 15th to the 19th centuries. The beautifully decorated private apartments include the dining room of Sultan Ahmet III, adorned with colorful paintings of flower arrangements and bowls of fruit.

DECORATED QUR'AN
This copy of the Qur'an, made in the 17th century in Delhi, India, has patterns picked out in gold leaf. Not all copies are as richly decorated as this, but when copying the Qur'an, Muslim calligraphers always try to make their script as beautiful as possible.

BRONZE BIRD
This small statuette of a bird is an example of the metalwork of Persia and dates from the 12th or 13th century. The patterns on the bird's wing and body are typical of the period.

WRITING BOX
Decorated with inlay and calligraphy, this writing box would have belonged to a very wealthy person. It contains pens, knives, brushes, inks, and other equipment for the calligrapher. The superb craftsmanship and luxurious materials of this object show the great importance placed on calligraphy in Islamic culture.

Ivory-handled knives

Brushes

PATTERNED RUG
The brightly colored patterns on this rug show how Islamic artists adapt shapes and other motifs from the natural world. The design is based on flowers, but they have been simplified, to give them a more abstract quality.

SUFIS

Sufism is the name given today to the spiritual way at the heart of Islam. Those who follow it have their own spiritual practices and a distinctive culture of poetry and music. Sufis aim to discover the inner meaning of Islam. They study under a spiritual teacher in order to come closer to Allah. Their practices sometimes include ecstatic singing and sacred dance rituals that have earned one group of Sufis the nickname "whirling dervishes".

TUNIC

The bold zigzag design on this tunic was made using a technique called *ikat*. *Ikat* involves tie-dyeing the threads before weaving. This method is used widely in Central Asia to produce bold, dramatic patterns.

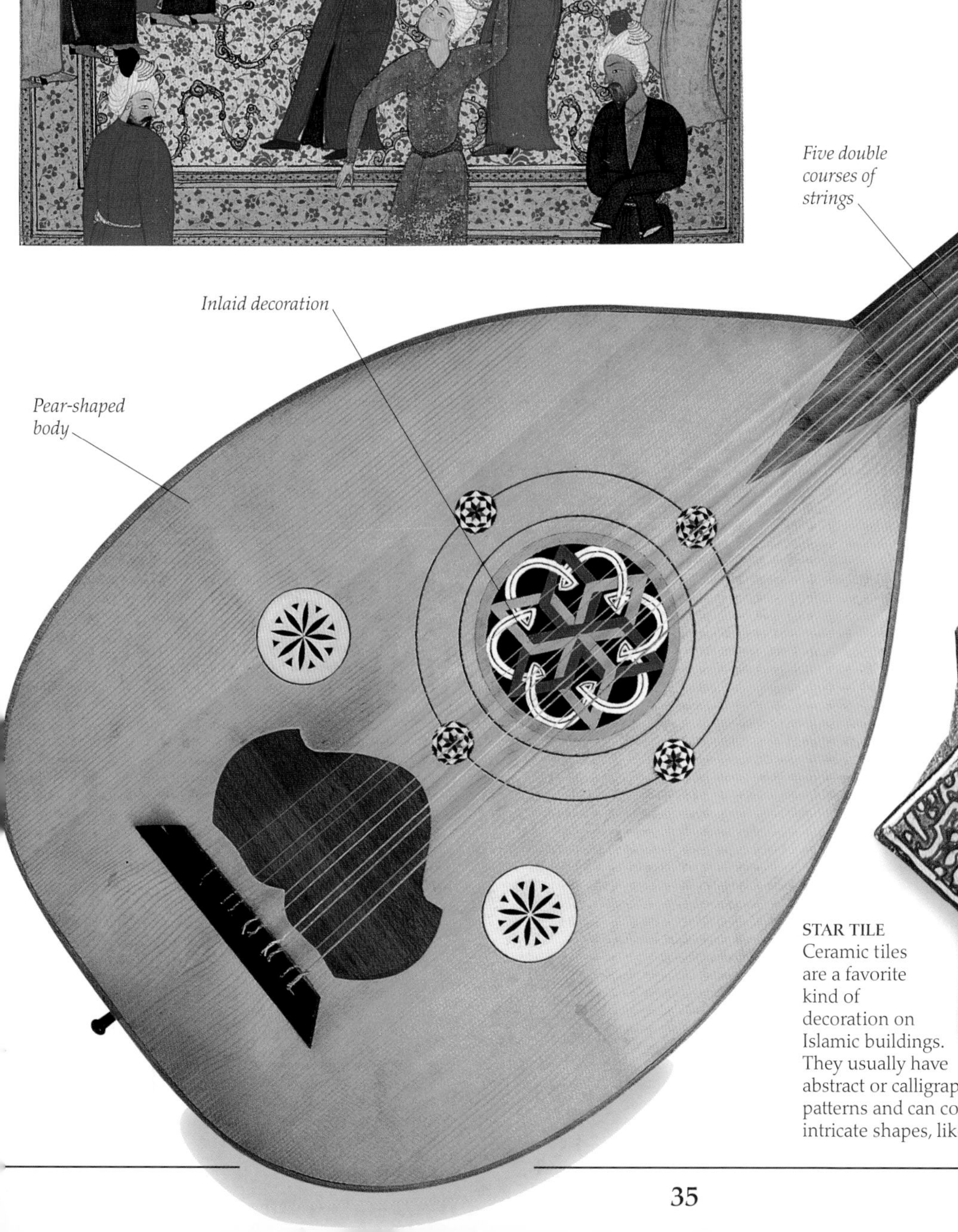

Five double courses of strings

Inlaid decoration

Pear-shaped body

LUTE

Arab music has its own instruments, and one of the most popular is the *'ud*, the ancestor of the Western lute. The *'ud* is used for both solos and playing in a group of instruments. Its warm sound, and the subtle effects that skilled players can produce, have earned the instrument the title *amir al-tarab* (prince of enchantment).

STAR TILE

Ceramic tiles are a favorite kind of decoration on Islamic buildings. They usually have abstract or calligraphic patterns and can come in intricate shapes, like this star.

The Islamic city

MUSLIMS INHERITED ideas about city planning from early civilizations such as ancient Rome, and they built large cities with facilities that were far in advance of those in Europe. A typical city in the year 1000 would have had a large mosque – usually with a school and library – and a market and baths. There were also caravanseries, which were hotels providing accommodation for traveling merchants and their animals.

Main mosque

City walls

Central square

WATER FOR SALE
Water sellers were a common sight in many Middle Eastern cities before reliable water supplies were installed. They can still be seen in some places.

Metal drinking cups

TOWN PLAN
Houses in an old Islamic city, such as Fez, were tightly packed, but each house had a private courtyard with a small garden and a fountain, as well as a flat rooftop. Many cities, especially in Turkey and Mughul India (pp. 52–53), had public gardens beyond the walls.

SEEKING A CURE
Medicine was advanced in the Muslim world (pp. 30–31) and some Islamic cities became renowned for their able doctors. Travelers would often return home with news of remarkable cures using remedies such as herbs and spices, and spread this knowledge further around the Islamic world and beyond.

MARKET PLACES
Suqs, or covered markets, are usually large, busy places. They are arranged so that shops selling similar goods are close together, so purchasers can compare quality and prices, and so that the official market inspectors (p. 58) can do their job effectively.

THE CITY GRAVEYARD
Burial places were usually outside the city walls. They were pleasant, green spaces with trees, which provided somewhere to walk, meditate, or enjoy the fresh air. Most people had simple graves, marked with a single stone.

Lookout tower gives a good vantage point and firing platform.

Battlements to conceal defenders

PUBLIC BATHS
Going to the baths was a social occasion – an opportunity to meet friends and exchange news – as well as a chance to get clean. This painting from Persia shows men visiting the baths. Women would use the baths at a different time of day.

TELLING A STORY
In some cities, comfortable coffee houses provided entertainment. People went to this coffee house in Istanbul both for refreshments and to while away the hours listening to the local storyteller.

PIGEON POST
Major Islamic cities were connected with an efficient postal service. Mail was transported by camels, mules, or horses, and in 1150, the Sultan of Baghdad even started a postal service using carrier pigeons.

City walls, Morocco

CITY WALLS
Walls enclosed many Muslim cities. They had to be strong enough to keep out attackers, give somewhere for defenders to stand safely, and provide a good view of the surrounding countryside. Gates could be locked to keep out enemies, or opened, when guards could keep an eye on who was entering and leaving the city.

WATERWHEELS
Bringing water into the city was sometimes a major task. In Hamah, Syria, two huge wooden waterwheels mounted on massive stone arches were built to raise water from the river to supply the town. Building wheels like this required great engineering skill.

Merchants and travellers

IBN BATTUTA
Among the early Muslim travelers, Ibn Battuta, from Tangier (in present-day Morocco), was the most remarkable. Setting out on the Pilgrimage in 1325, he continued traveling, going 75,000 miles (120,000 km) in 29 years. He visited West and East Africa, Arabia, India, and China, and when he returned he told the story of his adventures to the Sultan of Morocco.

TRADE HAS ALWAYS played a key role in the Islamic world. The Prophet himself came from a people who had long ago established the two great caravan journeys from Mecca, the Winter Caravan to the Yemen and the Summer Caravan to the outskirts of the Roman Empire. When Muslim armies took over territory, traders were quick to follow, opening up routes that led east to China, south into Africa, northwest to Europe, and southeast across the Indian Ocean. The faith of Islam was soon spread by merchants as far as Malaysia and Indonesia. Muslims did not only travel for trade, they also went in search of knowledge, on diplomatic missions, and of course to make the Pilgrimage.

MERCHANTS ON THE MOVE
This 13th-century illustration of merchants comes from a book by the writer al-Hariri, who came from Basra, Iraq. Men like these didn't just carry items for sale; they also carried ideas, inventions, and Islam itself, which was often introduced to new areas by merchants who settled far from home.

Silver coins from Baghdad found in a Viking grave in Sweden

Islamic trade routes

COINS FOR TRADE
Archeologists have found out where Islamic traders went by unearthing their coins. The Viking lands, Sri Lanka, and the heart of China are three places where Muslim coins have been discovered. Islamic coins were widely respected because of the high proportion of precious metals they contained. These currencies greatly helped the growth of world trade.

TRADE ROUTES
Official reports, travelers' tales, and archeology have all provided clues about the routes taken by Muslim traders. One route stood out above all – the Silk Road. It was actually a number of roads across Central Asia, linking China and Europe, passing through many parts of the Muslim world on the way.

SALT CARAVAN
This salt caravan is traveling to Timbuktu in Mali (p. 48). Salt was essential for seasoning and preserving food, and early Muslims sold it for vast sums. There were rich sources of salt in Africa, at places such as Taghaza, today in Algeria, where the locals even constructed buildings from salt. From here, caravans carried salt south, and the merchants spread Islam as they traveled.

DHOW

The most common trading vessels in the Indian Ocean were dhows, which are still used today. With their triangular sails, these boats are easy to maneuver and sail in headwinds. Their captains navigated by looking at the stars and many of them also used the magnetic compass. They also had an excellent knowledge of currents, sea-marks, and winds.

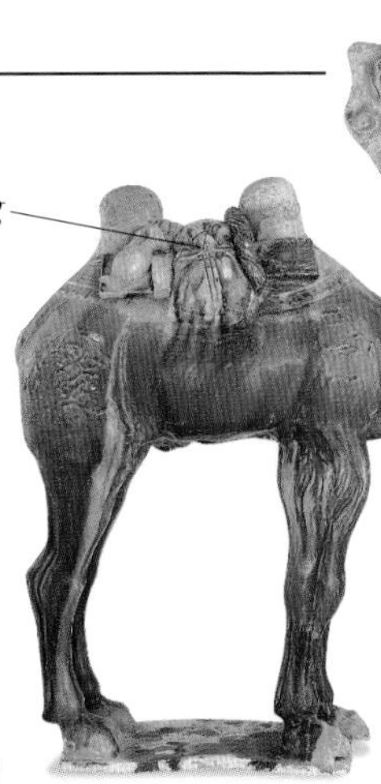

Tasseled saddlebag

BACTRIAN CAMEL

With their great staying power and their ability to produce milk on a diet of bitter vegetation and foul-tasting water, camels enabled the Muslims to survive and travel in inhospitable places. The two-humped Bactrian camel was found on the northern routes, the one-humped dromedary in the south.

Ropes help support mast

Furled lateen (triangular) sail

Main mast

CANDY FOR SALE

In countries such as Saudi Arabia, stores and markets have extremely enticing candy counters. For centuries, the Arab world has had a reputation for its confectioneries, and English words such as "sugar" and "candy" come from Arabic.

NOMAD WOMAN SPINNING

This painting shows an Egyptian livestock herder and his wife outside their tent. The woman is spinning wool to make thread. She uses some of this to make clothes for herself and her family. What is left over can be sold at a local market.

Stern rudder

Continued on next page

FRANKINCENSE
A resin from trees growing in southern Arabia, frankincense is burned for its perfume and was also an ingredient in medieval medicines. Frankincense was in great demand in Christian Europe because it was used in religious services. It became a major trading item for Muslim merchants.

NARWHAL TUSKS
Among the marvels on sale in medieval markets were tusks taken from the narwhal, a small species of whale. Stories of the unicorn, the mythical beast with a single horn, fascinated people in the Middle Ages and unscrupulous traders claimed that narwhal tusks were unicorn horns.

HUNTING BIRDS
Nobles in both East and West enjoyed hunting with falcons, and the Arab world produced some of the best, and most expensive, birds. When Muslim envoys visited the Chinese emperor during the Ming dynasty, he asked them to bring him falcons.

Exotic goods

The Muslim world had two enormous business advantages. Muslim merchants had a huge range of contacts over land and sea, so they could trade in everything from African gold and Chinese porcelain to European amber and furs. Muslim craft workers were also highly skilled, so merchants could bring back raw materials, which workers then transformed into all kinds of items – leather goods, metalwork, textiles, glass – that always found a ready market.

COTTON
Grown originally in Egypt and Iraq, cotton was a popular material for clothing because it was cool, comfortable, and cheaper than linen.

Cotton plant

OILS
Used in cooking, for soaps and cosmetics, and in lamps like this, oil was traded widely. The fine plant-based oils of the Muslim world were far more pleasant to use than the smelly fish oil that was often found in Europe.

CAMEL CARAVAN
Before modern forms of transportation appeared, camel caravans, each beast loaded with bags containing trade goods, were a common sight in Arabia, the Sahara, and on the Silk Road across Asia.

Robe dyed using indigo

DYES
Blue was a very popular color for fabrics and there was a valuable trade in indigo, a blue dye made from plants and used today in clothes such as denim jeans. Other dyes, such as Roman purple made from murex shellfish, were rarer and more expensive.

SILKS
Muslim merchants brought silk yarns and finished fabrics from China along the Silk Road (p. 38). The yarns were woven into cloth in cities such as Damascus (which gave us the word damask), in Syria, and sold on to Western traders.

Silk fabric

THE IVORY TRADE
Elephant ivory was brought across the Sahara and through Ethiopia to be exported from the ports of North Africa. Much of it went to Muslim Spain, where craft workers produced stunning ivory objects, such as decorated horns and intricately carved caskets.

Oyster shell with pearl

PEARL FISHING
Diving for pearls was dangerous work, but divers risked their lives in the fine pearl beds of the Arabian Gulf and Indian Ocean because of the huge demand. There were thriving pearl markets in Bahrain, Sri Lanka, and around the Strait of Hormuz, between Oman and Iran.

Pearl necklace

Elephant ivory

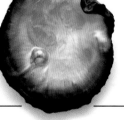

Food trade

The Muslim world developed a vigorous trade in various types of foods, and this business still continues today. The trade was beneficial in several ways. Not only was there great financial gain for the merchants, but Western Europe was also introduced to foodstuffs from all over Asia. Without Muslim merchants, Europeans would have had no rice, sugar, or coffee. In addition, the merchants set up trading colonies in many parts of the world, and this helped Islam to spread eastward as far as Southeast Asia.

Thai rice pot

Cinnamon sticks

Peppercorns

Ginger

Nutmeg

RICE
The Muslims brought rice from Southeast Asia and it soon became a popular food in parts of Europe. Later, Western growers learned how to grow rice for themselves.

THE FRUIT TRADE
Muslim travelers introduced new species of fruit, such as the apricot, into Europe. Dried fruit, such as dates, kept for a long time and could be carried for months. Fresh fruit did not travel so well, although highly valued melons were sometimes wrapped in lead to preserve them.

Cherries

PRECIOUS SPICES
Grown on the islands of Indonesia, spices fetched high prices in Europe and western Asia, where they were used in both food and medicines. From the time of Muhammad until the 16th century, Muslim merchants ran the spice trade, bringing nutmeg, cloves, cinnamon, and other spices to Arabia by sea and selling them at a huge profit to European traders.

Cloves

Apricots

Figs

Dates

Bedouin bag for coffee beans and cardamom pods

Tea leaves

Green coffee beans

SUGAR
A great luxury in the Middle Ages, sugar was brought west from Iran and Iraq to Muslim Spain. Access to this expensive ingredient gave Muslim confectioners the chance to create their own specialities – sherbet from Persia, various types of candy, sweets made from the liquorice plant, and Turkish delight – all of which eventually reached Europe through trade.

Sherbet

Boiled candies

TEA AND COFFEE
India and China were sources of tea, while coffee was grown in Yemen and traded from the town of Mocha, which gave its name to a type of high-quality coffee. Both drinks came late to world trade but became very fashionable in the 18th century.

Turkish delight

Liquorice

Sugared almonds

The crusades

THE CITY OF JERUSALEM is sacred to followers of three faiths – Islam, Christianity, and Judaism. From the seventh century, Jerusalem and the surrounding area were ruled by Muslims, who had mostly lived in harmony with the Christians and Jews of the city. But in the late 11th century, the Christian Byzantine Empire, based in Turkey on the pilgrimage route to Jerusalem, was at war with the Muslim Seljuk Turks, and Christian pilgrims reported difficulties in visiting Jerusalem. The Europeans launched a series of largely unsuccessful wars called the crusades to try and defeat the Muslims and take over Jerusalem and other nearby lands.

PREACHING THE CRUSADE
In 1095, Pope Urban II preached at Clermont, France. He called for a Christian army to capture Jerusalem. A number of European lords saw this as an opportunity to create power bases in and around the city.

SELJUK BOWL
In the 11th century, Turkish warriors called the Seljuks, portrayed on this painted bowl, ruled a Muslim empire that stretched from Iran and Iraq to the eastern Mediterranean.

ENGINE OF BATTLE
The crusades involved many sieges when the European armies attacked fortified cities such as Antioch and Damascus. These attacks were often ruthless, bloodthirsty assaults, and the crusaders sometimes used powerful, outsize weapons, like this giant crossbow, when besieging Muslim cities.

Winding mechanism to pull back string

Bolt ready to fire

Handle for aiming crossbow

INTO THE BATTLE
In the first crusade (1096–99), a number of French and Norman knights, such as Godfrey of Bouillon, took armies to Jerusalem. After numerous battles with the Muslims, they were able to set up small kingdoms for themselves in the East.

Painting of battling Christians and Muslims

JERUSALEM
The first crusade ended when Jerusalem fell to the Europeans in July 1099, and Count Baldwin of Flanders was crowned king of the city. Christians remained in power here for over 80 years.

KRAK DES CHEVALIERS

The European knights who occupied the Holy Land during the crusades built impressive castles as military bases. The strongest and biggest of these castles was Krak des Chevaliers in Syria. It was rebuilt by French knights in the early 12th century, and its massive walls kept out many attackers.

Tall tower gives good lookout position

Aqueduct for water supply

Wooden wheel

RICHARD "THE LIONHEART"

This English king was one of the leaders of the third crusade (1188–92). Although he was a brave fighter and captured Acre, the crusade was badly organized and achieved little.

Illustration from a 13th-century French manuscript *Historia Major*

SALADIN'S LEGACY

Saladin, who is buried in this tomb in Damascus, Syria, was a fearless fighter who was always just to his enemies. He built up an empire in Syria, Palestine, and Egypt, and founded the Ayyubid dynasty, which ruled until 1260.

SALADIN

Salah ad-Din, known in the West as Saladin, was a Muslim leader who fought a *jihad* (a struggle in accordance with strict limitations set out in the Qur'an) against the crusaders under Richard the Lionheart. In 1187, he recaptured Jerusalem, which would remain under Muslim rule for the next 800 years.

THE MAMLUKS

The Mamluks were originally slaves who were recruited to fight for the Muslims. Eventually they became a military ruling class, defeating Christians in the later crusades. After overthrowing the Ayyubids in the 13th century, they ruled their own empire for over 250 years.

Arms and armor

BY THE 11TH CENTURY, Muslims were highly skilled in metal craftsmanship – and this included weapon production. For a fighting man, good arms and armor were often a matter of life and death, so soldiers wanted the best equipment that they could afford. The mounted warriors of the Islamic world used the sword, lance, and mace. Most were also skilled archers. Beautiful and intricate swords, shields, and other weaponry were the envy of the non-Muslim world. However, Muslim armies were also quick to adopt weapons that originated in the West, such as cannons and firearms.

CANNON MINIATURE
By the early 14th century, European armorers were starting to make cannons and these powerful weapons were quickly taken up by Muslim armies. This painting shows cannons being used by Muslim troops at the Siege of Vienna in 1529.

TURKISH HELMET
This Turkish helmet dates from around 1500. It is made of iron and patterned with silver. It carries the mark of the "Arsenal of Constantinople" (now Istanbul) where the weapons and armor of the Turkish army were held.

19th-century Indian steel shield with gilt decoration

SHIELD OF STEEL
The Mongols developed small, round shields made of leather. When enemy archers fired, their arrows stuck in the leather and could be pulled out and reused. Later round shields were made of steel with a curving surface, to protect the user from both bullets and sword blows. Shields like this were popular in India and Iran from the 18th century onward.

Sword and sheath of Shah Tamasp of Persia

Handle hides a slender dagger.

GRENADE
First used in China, grenades containing gunpowder were used by both Muslims and Christians in the Middle Ages. This 13th-century example was made of clay in Damascus, Syria.

MACE
Maces were sometimes carried as a sign of rank, but they were also fighting weapons used by mounted warriors. In skilled hands, a mace could break an opponent's bones, even if he was wearing armor.

Steel mace from Persia

Jambiya (and sheath, below right)

Khanjar and decorated sheath

KHANJAR
In many parts of the Muslim world it was common for men, and even boys, to carry weapons. This is a 20th-century dagger from Yemen, called a *khanjar*.

JAMBIYA
First made in the Arabian Peninsula, the *jambiya* was a curved dagger. It proved popular – either as a plain fighting dagger or as an ornate ceremonial weapon – and spread all over the Muslim world.

SHOOTING LESSON
Handheld guns first appeared in Western Europe in the 15th century and Muslim soldiers soon began to use them. It was not long before Muslim craft workers started to make such weapons for themselves, often in workshops run by master-armorers from Portugal. In this picture, 16th century Indian Emperor Akbar is learning how to handle one of the latest weapons.

Gold-barreled musket

MUSKET
When they were first imported to the East, guns like this European flintlock musket were resisted by high-ranking Muslim soldiers, who preferred the bow and the curved sword. But when their enemies began to take up firearms, Muslim warriors were forced to do the same, and weapons like the musket were valued all over Asia.

SWORDS AND BATTLE-AXES
The tabar, or battle-ax, was a widespread weapon. Such axes had steel blades and were not always as ornate as this one, which is adorned with silver and gilding. Muslim soldiers also fought with distinctive swords with curved blades that broadened toward the tip. In Europe these were known as scimitars (above).

Spain

DURING THE EARLY EIGHTH century, Muslims from Morocco invaded Spain – soon they controlled most of the Iberian Peninsula. Muslims ruled in Spain until the 15th century, although they never governed the entire peninsula, as Christian kingdoms survived in the north. After the fall of the caliphate in the 11th century, Moorish Spain began to be conquered by the Christians of the north and the east, but southern cities such as Cordoba and Seville were centers of Islamic art and learning.

MOORISH COIN
The Moors – the name Christians gave to the Muslims from Morocco – brought with them their own coinage and systems of government. After the defeat of the Moors, early Spanish Christian kings continued to use Islamic designs on coins.

GREAT MOSQUE AT CORDOBA
Begun in the ninth century and later extended, the Great Mosque, or Mezquita, in Cordoba was a symbol of Muslim power in Spain. It is a dazzling example of Islamic architecture. Over 850 columns of granite, jasper, and marble support a ceiling raised on double arches.

MINSTRELS
The musicians of Muslim Spain were among the best in Europe. Some of them were wandering minstrels who introduced European players to the lute, and to the use of the bow to play stringed instruments.

THE ALHAMBRA, GRANADA
In the 14th century, Spain was ruled by the Nasrid dynasty who were based in Granada, in southern Spain. Here they built the great fortified palace called the Alhambra, which means "red palace," after the warm color of its stone. It was designed to represent paradise on Earth and its tall towers and strong outer walls hide luxurious interiors.

CALIPH'S BOX
A great Moorish craftsman produced this box during the 10th century. It is inscribed with the name of Al-Mughira, son of 'Abd al-Rahman III, who reunited Islamic Spain after a time of disorder and ruled as Caliph of Cordoba.

Scenes showing pleasures of courtly life

ALHAMBRA COURTYARDS
The beauty of the Alhambra lies not only in its exquisite Islamic decoration, but in the clever use of light and water to create a sense of space. Courtyards fill the palace with light, and many have tranquil pools that gently reflect the light. Arched walkways create shaded areas where the Nasrids could walk or relax.

MUDEJAR TOWER
In many parts of Spain, Muslim craftsmen carried on working under Christian rule. They developed a style, now known as *mudéjar*, which used Islamic patterns to decorate brick-built wall surfaces, as in this tower at Teruel.

THE GARDENS OF THE GENERALIFE
In the Qur'an, paradise is described as a garden – usually an enclosed or shaded garden in which water flows. To escape from the political life of the palace, the Nasrid caliphs created a tranquil garden paradise on their country estate, the Generalife, which looked down over the city of Granada.

THE LAST MUSLIM KINGDOM
As the Christians gradually conquered Spain, the Muslim rulers were pushed south. By the 15th century, only the kingdom of Granada, the area in southern Spain around the walled city of the same name, remained in Muslim hands.

THE LAST CALIPH
Boabdil became caliph in 1482, after a power struggle with his father that weakened Granada. In 1490, the Christian forces of Aragon and Castille laid siege to the city and, after two years, Granada surrendered. On his way to exile in Morocco, Boabdil looked back at the Alhambra and wept at its beauty. This spot is now called "the Moor's last sigh."

MOORISH INFLUENCE
This metalwork decorates a door in the royal palace in Seville. The palace was not built by a caliph but by a Spanish king, Pedro I, and shows the great influence of Islamic art in Spain.

Africa

By the end of the Umayyad dynasty of caliphs in 750, Islam had spread across North Africa from Egypt to Morocco. From here, the faith spread southward, as Muslim Berber and Tuareg merchants crossed Africa carrying not just goods, but also ideas. Great cities of Islamic scholarship were established at Timbuktu and Djenne (both in Mali) and Chingetti, in Mauritania. Today Muslims – most of them Sunnis – are in the majority in North and West Africa, and many East African countries. Africa is a vast and varied continent, in which Islam exists side by side with many different local cultures and with political systems that range from socialism to monarchy.

WOMAN WARRIOR
One of the best known accounts of the Muslim conquests in North Africa is an epic called the *Sirat Beni Hilal*. One especially popular character is the heroine Jazia, a warrior who is shown here riding her camel.

BERBER WOMAN
The Berbers are the peoples of the mountains and deserts of North Africa. They are Muslims who have held on to many of their local traditions, such as wearing bright-colored costumes and silver jewelry.

Wide margin allows the pages to be turned without touching the text.

ILLUMINATED COPY OF THE QUR'AN
Calligraphy and other scholarly skills were as highly valued in Africa as in the rest of the Muslim world, and Africa had some famous centers of learning. One of the largest of these was 15th- and 16th-century Timbuktu. Scholars from all over North Africa came to the city's library to consult precious manuscripts like this copy of the Qur'an.

Earth pinnacle built around wooden post

DJENNE MOSQUE
Earth is the traditional building material in many parts of Africa. In addition to being used for houses, large buildings, like this mosque at Djenne in Mali, can be made of earth. Djenne was one of the most important trading centers along the Niger River.

MINARET AT SOUSSE
When the Muslim conquerors took over areas like Tunisia, they founded cities and built mosques in which to pray. The ninth-century mosque at Sousse, with its round stone minaret, is one early example.

WEARING THE QUR'AN
This tunic was worn by a warrior of the Asante people of West Africa. The pouches each contain a text from the Qur'an, which warriors believed would protect them in battle.

Leather pouch containing verse from the Qur'an

TILE PATTERNS
These hexagonal wall tiles from North Africa bear patterns that are based on plant forms. The flowers, leaves, and twining stems have been made into abstract designs in typical Islamic style.

PRECIOUS METAL
The people of West Africa were skilled gold workers before the arrival of Islam. The Muslims put these skills to work to produce gold coinage.

MEMORIZING THE QUR'AN
Islam brought formal education to many parts of Africa for the first time. This Mauritanian student is reading a *sura* (chapter) of the Qur'an, and learning it by heart.

A FAMOUS PILGRIMAGE
Mali was the center of a large West African empire during the 14th century. Its ruler, Mansa Musa, made the pilgrimage to Mecca in 1324–25, and his long journey is recorded on this map.

Smooth outer coating of mud protects walls.

Wooden beams strengthen the structure.

DOMED TOMB
Most Muslims have simple graves, but there is a tradition of building larger tombs for caliphs and other notable people. The small tomb above, near Khartoum in Sudan, was probably built for a local saint. It is marked by a simple dome so that people can visit to pay their respects.

Mongols and Turks

In 1219 THE LANDS OF ISLAM were invaded by Mongol armies from the north. By 1258, the Mongols – great warriors from the steppes of Mongolia – had sacked Baghdad and killed the caliph, devastating Islam's political center. But in 1260, the Mongols were defeated by the Mamluks, and many converted to Islam. The next great Muslim power was the Ottoman empire, founded by the Turks in 1290. They conquered part of Eastern Europe and, like the Arabs before them, became the dominant political force in Islam.

GENGHIS KHAN
Genghis Khan was a Mongol warlord who came to power in 1206 when he succeeded in uniting warring Mongol tribes. He then began a campaign of raiding and conquest. At his death in 1227, his empire stretched from China to the borders of Europe.

MONGOL SOLDIER
The Mongol warriors were skilled horsemen and ruthless fighters. Moving at great speed, they killed millions and destroyed hundreds of settlements to bring much of Asia under the control of Mongol rulers.

WARRIOR BOWL
The Mongols were proud of their warriors, as this decorated bowl from the ninth century shows. Because they began as a nomadic people, the Mongols' detailed knowledge of the land meant that they were able to vanish into the countryside, reappearing again suddenly to take their enemies by surprise.

THE NEW MONGOL CAPITAL
After the death of Genghis Khan, his empire was divided between his three sons and his grandson, Kublai Khan. The eastern empire prospered under Kublai Khan, and he founded the Yüan dynasty in China where he built a new capital, called Khanbaliq, now Beijing.

Embroidered cloth

Pillar of skulls

THE RUTHLESS TIMUR
Perhaps the cruelest of all the Mongol conquerors was Timur, or Tamerlane. He was a Turkish-Mongol leader who claimed to be a descendant of Genghis Khan. In the 14th century he conquered much of the western part of the Mongol empire, taking Baghdad in 1390. He liked to display his victims' skulls after major battles and this painting, of his victory at Baghdad, shows a gruesome tower of skulls.

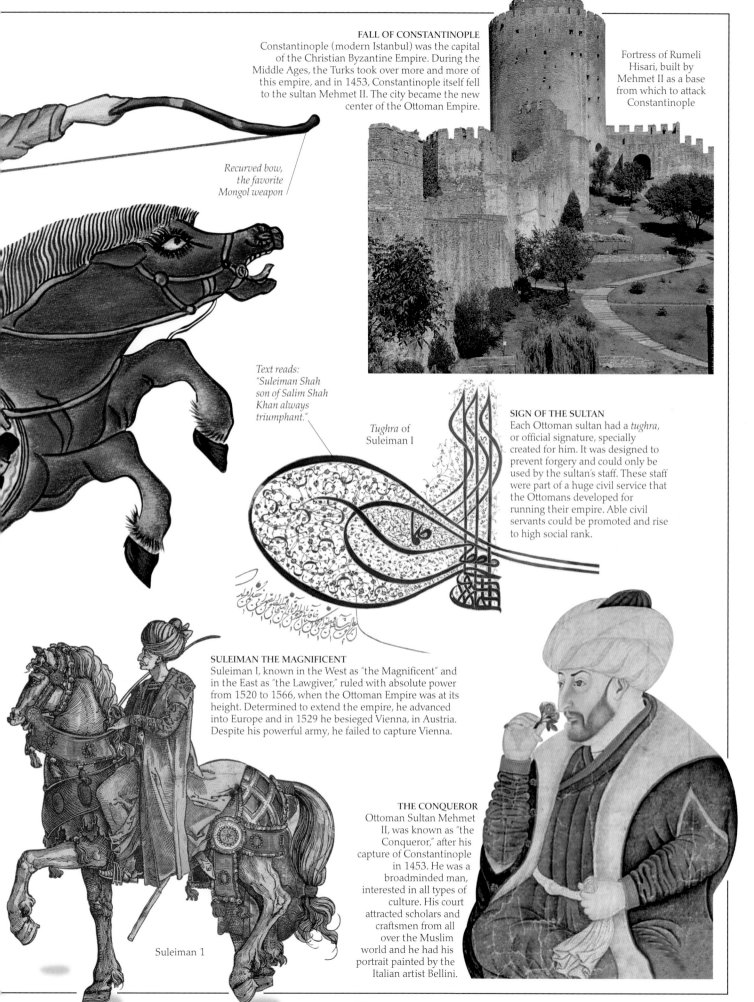

FALL OF CONSTANTINOPLE

Constantinople (modern Istanbul) was the capital of the Christian Byzantine Empire. During the Middle Ages, the Turks took over more and more of this empire, and in 1453, Constantinople itself fell to the sultan Mehmet II. The city became the new center of the Ottoman Empire.

Fortress of Rumeli Hisari, built by Mehmet II as a base from which to attack Constantinople

Recurved bow, the favorite Mongol weapon

Text reads: "Suleiman Shah son of Salim Shah Khan always triumphant."

Tughra of Suleiman I

SIGN OF THE SULTAN

Each Ottoman sultan had a *tughra*, or official signature, specially created for him. It was designed to prevent forgery and could only be used by the sultan's staff. These staff were part of a huge civil service that the Ottomans developed for running their empire. Able civil servants could be promoted and rise to high social rank.

SULEIMAN THE MAGNIFICENT

Suleiman I, known in the West as "the Magnificent" and in the East as "the Lawgiver," ruled with absolute power from 1520 to 1566, when the Ottoman Empire was at its height. Determined to extend the empire, he advanced into Europe and in 1529 he besieged Vienna, in Austria. Despite his powerful army, he failed to capture Vienna.

Suleiman 1

THE CONQUEROR

Ottoman Sultan Mehmet II, was known as "the Conqueror," after his capture of Constantinople in 1453. He was a broadminded man, interested in all types of culture. His court attracted scholars and craftsmen from all over the Muslim world and he had his portrait painted by the Italian artist Bellini.

Central Asia, Iran, and India

BURNING BRIGHT
The Ghaznavids, whose craftsmen made elaborate metalwork like this lamp, were Seljuk rulers who controlled Afghanistan and much of Iran. They were at the height of their power in the early 11th century. The Ghaznavids were Sunni Muslims who opposed the rival Shi'i dynasty, the Buyids, in Iran.

Pierced decoration

Lamp is made of cast bronze

I{SLAM CAME EARLY TO IRAN}, an area that was completely conquered by Muslim rulers by the year 641. In the following centuries, a series of ruling dynasties reigned in Iran, including the Seljuks from Turkey, the Mongols from Central Asia, the Timurids (the dynasty of the war leader Timur), and the Safavids. India was also a region of huge variety, with many different religions. Muslims – from the first conquests in Sind in 712 to the Mughal emperors – controlled all or part of India from 1193 to the 19th century, when the subcontinent became part of the vast British Empire. When the country won its independence from Britain in 1947, it was split up and the new Muslim state of Pakistan was created. A growing Muslim minority remains in India.

QUTB MINAR, DELHI
In 1193, Afghan ruler Muhammad al-Ghuri conquered northern India. He built a capital at Delhi from which Muslim sultans ruled, putting up buildings like this tall minaret. For the most part, the rule of the Delhi sultans was ended by the campaigns of Timur in 1398–9, but carried on in some areas until 1526.

TIMUR'S TOMB
The Mongol war leader Timur (p. 50) was a highly successful soldier who had victories in Iran, India, Syria, and Turkey. When he died in 1405, he was trying to add China to his list of military triumphs. The great wealth he amassed from his conquests is reflected by the rich decoration of his tomb at Samarkand in Central Asia.

FRIDAY MOSQUE, ISFAHAN
Isfahan, Iran, was the capital of the powerful Safavid dynasty (1501–1732), which unified the area and made Shi'i Islam the state religion. The Safavid sultans built a series of stunning buildings in the city, including a large palace complex, several mosques, and the large Friday Mosque. The red-and-blue glazed tilework of the 16th and 17th centuries is in typical Safavid style.

KHWAJU BRIDGE
One of the achievements of the Safavid dynasty was the construction of the Khwaju Bridge in Isfahan. The bridge is about 440 ft (133 m) long and spans the Zayandeh River with 23 arches. In addition to providing a river crossing, this amazing structure acted as a dam to irrigate the nearby gardens.

Openings allow passersby to enjoy river views in the shade.

The Mughal empire

The Muslim Mughal dynasty ruled in India from 1526 to 1858, with the greatest emperors in power toward the beginning of this period. Under their rule, the diverse Indian subcontinent was united and underwent a unique period of achievement in art, music, literature and architecture. Under the later Mughal rulers, however, the empire began to fall apart.

Babur discusses building progress with his architects

BABUR

The first Mughal emperor was Babur, who came from Iran and was descended from Timur and Genghis Khan. The word Mughal comes from "Mongol," because of Babur's origins. Babur was just 11 when he became a ruler in Transoxiana, and aged 14 when he conquered Samarkand. He established a kingdom in Iran, which he lost, and another in Afghanistan. In 1526, Babur conquered India. A well-educated man, he was a poet and historian who encouraged the arts.

Akbar leads his army into battle

AKBAR

The greatest Mughal emperor was Akbar, who ruled from 1556 to 1605. Skilled in government, Akbar set up an efficient bureaucracy, the structure of which still influences Indian government today. Akbar was also known as one of the most tolerant of rulers. He abolished a tax on the Hindu population, and encouraged artists to combine Hindu and Islamic styles in their work.

AURANGZEB

This book contains the letters of the last important Mughal leader, emperor Aurangzeb (1658–1070), whose rule saw a decline in the health of the Mughal state. He expanded the empire but failed to invest in agriculture and so did not make enough money to support his army or court. He persecuted non-Muslims, taxing Hindus heavily and destroying many of their temples.

China and Southeast Asia

ISLAM HAS BEEN PRACTICED in China since the seventh century when it was introduced to coastal cities by Arab traders. Over the next 200 years, merchants traveling the Silk Road took Islam into the interior. The Muslims of China today are a diverse people descended from many different ethnic groups, including ethnic Chinese, Mongols, and Persians, each with their own customs and cultures. Islam also reached Southeast Asia through trade, and today the largest Muslim population in the world is in Indonesia.

BY SEA
Some Muslim merchants traveled from the mainland to Southeast Asia in traditional boats with striking curved prows.

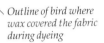
Name of Allah

Outline of bird where wax covered the fabric during dyeing

BATIK
China and Southeast Asia have always traded in beautiful fabrics, such as silks. This piece has been dyed using the process called batik, which was invented in Java. The dyer applies wax to the parts of the fabric which are to remain uncolored, then soaks the material in dye. When dry, the material is boiled or scraped to remove the wax.

Typical Chinese upward-curving roof

Carved stone decoration from Xi'an mosque

MOSQUE INTERIOR, BEIJING
By the early 20th century there was a sizeable Muslim minority in China. In the larger cities there are lavish mosques like the Niu Jie mosque (above), which has pillars lacquered in black and gold, and walls decorated with both Arabic and Chinese motifs. Most of China's Muslims live in the rural northwestern province of Xinjiang, where the mosques are usually much plainer.

GRAND MOSQUE IN THE CITY OF XI'AN,
When China became communist in 1949, Muslims were given some religious freedom, but during the Cultural Revolution (1966–1976) all religions were outlawed, and mosques were destroyed or closed. In the 1980s, however, many mosques were reopened or rebuilt. China's oldest mosque, the Grand Mosque in Xi'an, can be visited today.

ROD PUPPET

The shadow puppet theater called *wayang golek* is performed with carved and painted wooden figures that are manipulated with rods. *Wayang* is a traditional Javanese entertainment, widely enjoyed by Muslims at festivals and celebrations.

Articulated arm

Wooden rod is used to move puppet's arm.

Clothing conceals stick used to hold puppet.

WEARING THE TUDONG

These schoolgirls from Brunei are wearing the *tudong*, a form of head-covering that extends down to conceal the neck and upper body. Wearing the *tudong* is just one way in which women can obey the Qur'an's instruction to dress modestly (p. 56).

BOWL FOR RICE

Rice is the staple food in both China and Southeast Asia. It is eaten from small round bowls made of porcelain – a type of pottery that was widely traded, forging an important link between China, the Muslim world, and the West.

MIX OF STYLES

This modern mosque in Kuala Kangsar, Malaysia, was built after the country became independent in 1957. This was a good time for Muslims in Malaysia because Islam was recognized as the state's official religion.

MALAYSIAN MOSQUE

Because Islam was brought to Southeast Asia by well-traveled merchants, the area has always been influenced by a mix of cultures. This Malaysian mosque is decorated in the style of mosques in Iran and India.

CARAVANSERAI

Merchants traveling by land needed places to stay, so the locals built caravanserais (p. 36) on the routes through Asia to China. In these simple stone buildings, merchants could find a bed and somewhere to stable their camels.

Costume and jewelry

THERE IS NO ONE Muslim style of dress, although the Qur'an instructs women and men to dress modestly. As a result, Muslims wear all types of different clothes, from the traditional garments of the Arabian desert to modern Western dress. A rich variety of traditional costumes is still worn today, particularly on special occasions such as family celebrations. These beautiful garments show how skills such as weaving, dyeing, and embroidery have been refined and handed on from one generation to the next throughout the Islamic world, from North Africa to eastern Asia.

AT SCHOOL
Many Muslim children wear modern dress, like these Chinese children in kindergarten. Only their headgear – the boys' caps and the girls' headdresses – differ from the kinds of clothes worn by children all over the world.

UZBEK BRIDE
In many places, wedding celebrations are a time to put on elaborate traditional costumes. This bride from Uzbekistan wears a gold headdress, a dress of rich fabrics woven with gold threads, and a long embroidered head-covering that falls almost to the floor.

COIN ROBE
In Arabia and western Asia it is an old custom to wear much of your wealth. This Bedouin robe has coins stitched to it. It is made of natural cotton, which is comfortable to wear in the desert heat.

Saudi Arabian woman wearing a face veil

THE VEIL
In some Muslim communities, it is traditional for women to veil their faces. The veil may cover the lower part of the face, up to the eyes, or may cover the whole face, as here.

A MODERN TWIST
Muslim boys often wear this type of brightly colored cap. The shape is traditional, as is the technique of embroidery used to decorate it. But the pattern can be modern, like the helicopter design used here.

GOLD BRACELET
Arab metalworkers pride themselves on their jewelry. For centuries, they worked mostly in silver, but now gold is a popular material for the bracelets and other pieces that are bought for a bride when she marries.

HEAD DECORATION
This is a traditional form of jewelry in the Arabian Peninsula. A woman wears a pair of head decorations, one over each ear.

Chains and roundels made of silver

AMULETS
Some Muslims carry an ornament or piece of jewelry to protect them from evil, called an amulet. This might be a stone carved with a verse from the Qur'an, or a box containing Qur'anic texts.

ENAMELED NECKLACE
Jewelry can be given bright red, blue, and green colors by enameling. This involves applying a mixture of powdered colored glass to the metalwork and heating the piece in a kiln to make the decoration hard and permanent.

CHINESE ROBE
Fine silks, often with added embroidered decoration, are among the most elegant of Chinese traditional garments. The example below has wide sleeves, which are typical of Oriental designs.

DAZZLING DESIGN
This North African robe shows two forms of bright, colorful decoration. The stripes are made by sewing different colored fabrics together. But what really makes the robe stand out is the encrustation of brilliantly colored beads.

TWO-WAY PATTERN
The outside of the Central Asian robe above is produced using the *ikat* technique (p. 35). The lining stands out as its flower patterns contrast well with the zigzag *ikat*.

Islamic society

THE QUR'AN TELLS MUSLIMS that man is God's vice regent on Earth and is responsible for taking good care of everything from the environment to the people around him. Muslims are told to be tolerant of other peoples and to create societies in which justice, personal kindness, and the avoidance of wrongdoing are upheld. Virtues such as these start within the family and the Qur'an describes clearly the roles of men, women, and children. Within these guidelines, which are known as the *sharia*, Muslim society can take a variety of forms.

SULTAN AND HIS SUBJECTS
Muslim countries are governed in different ways. In the past, many had heads of state who ruled with absolute power, like this Moroccan sultan. Since World War II and the abolition of the caliphate (p. 20), most Muslims now live in modern nation states.

SELLING SLAVES
Slavery had been an important part of the social system since ancient times, and was still common in the time of Muhammad. It continued to be a part of life in medieval times as this picture of a North African slave market shows. The Qur'an encouraged the freeing of slaves and insisted that they be treated with kindness.

SCALES OF JUSTICE
Islamic law also covers business, encouraging trade, but setting guidelines that ensure fairness. Since Abbasid times (p. 20), markets in Muslim countries have had officials who checked weights and measures and the quality of merchandise. The *Muhtasib*, as this public official was called, is still found in some traditional markets.

"Allah created nothing finer on Earth than justice. Justice is Allah's balance on Earth, and any man who upholds this balance will be carried by Him to Paradise."

THE PROPHET MUHAMMAD

TOLERANCE
The Qur'an stresses that there should be tolerance between Muslims and non-Muslims. Jews and Christians, people who, like Muslims, believe in the One God, are given particular respect in the Qur'an. They should be able to coexist peacefully, like the Muslim and Christian chessplayers in this Spanish picture.

MARCHING TOGETHER
Many Muslims live side by side with people of very different beliefs. For the most part, they live in harmony, like these Muslims and Buddhists in China.

SPIRES AND MINARETS
In Zanzibar, Tanzania, the mosque and the Christian church are close neighbors. Here, as in many places, Muslims live in a diverse community, side by side with Christians and those who follow other religions.

MEN'S ROLE
Islam makes a clear distinction between the roles of men and women in the home. The man's job is to deal with relations between the family and the outside world, as this man is doing when he entertains his guests.

CHILDREN AND FAMILY
Muslims regard children as gifts of Allah and as one of the great joys of life. Parents are expected to care for their children and to give them a good start in life, making sure they have a proper upbringing and education. Children are expected to respect and obey their parents and to show qualities of kindness, virtue, and conscientiousness toward them.

HENNAED HAND
Henna is used in a traditional ritual that is usually performed on the day before a marriage. The bride's hands and feet are adorned with beautiful patterns using a dye made from henna leaves. This may be done by the bride's female friends and relatives.

MARRIED LIFE
Muslims are usually expected to marry and have children. Marriage not only unites individuals, but it also brings together families, making the Muslim community more unified and reflecting the harmony of Allah's creation.

DOWRY BOX
A Muslim man gives his bride-to-be a dowry, a payment in money or property, which may be presented in a box like this. The amount of the dowry can vary according to the man's wealth.

Pattern is said to symbolize strength and love.

WESTERN WOMEN
In many societies, Muslim women are educated to a high level, are employed in professions such as medicine or law, and may even take a prominent part in public life. Baroness Uddin, a Muslim member of the British House of Lords, is a good example.

SUDANESE WOMAN
In traditional Muslim societies such as Sudan, women usually keep to their roles of homemaking and childcare. Even in early Muslim societies, however, there were notable women who worked as scholars and occasionally ruled. Many learned Muslim women, such as the great Egyptian scholar Umm Hani (1376–1466), were famous in the Middle Ages.

Local terra-cotta pot

MAN AT PRAYER
According to Islam, everything comes from Allah and will eventually return to Allah. Qualities that are loved in family members, friends, and the wider society are all qualities that have come from Allah. So the individual's relationship with Allah is paramount. Each Muslim turns to Allah for guidance, forgiveness, and support.

Festivals and ceremonies

THE MUSLIM CALENDAR contains a number of yearly festivals. Some commemorate key events in the history of the faith, such as the birthday of the Prophet or the Night Journey. Others are connected with the Five Pillars of Islam: *'Id al-Adha* (the feast of the sacrifice) takes place during the time of the pilgrimage, and *'Id al-Fitr* marks the end of Ramadan, the month of fasting. There are also festivals such as *Nauruz* in Iran to celebrate the New Year, and celebrations, from birth to marriage, to mark key points in a Muslim's life.

LUNAR CALENDAR
The Islamic calendar is based on the phases of the Moon. Each year has 12 lunar months of 29 or 30 days each, and a total of 354 days. Each month begins with the sighting of the new Moon.

KERBALA
Kerbala, Iraq, is where Muhammad's grandson Husayn was killed in 680. Husayn's shrine (above) is sacred to the Shi'i Muslims, who are the largest religious group in Iran and Iraq. The death of Husayn is marked by the festival of *Ashura* (see opposite).

RAMADAN
During the month of Ramadan, Muslims fast between sunrise and sunset (p.15). At sunset each day, people first pray and then eat. Special lights, such as this star-shaped lantern, may be lit during the evening meal.

MAWLID AN-NABI
These boys from Kenya are taking part in a procession celebrating *Mawlid an-Nabi*, the birthday of the Prophet. This day is a public holiday and is also marked with recitations of a poem called the *Burdah*, in praise of Muhammad.

"EID MUBARAK"
During the festival of *'Id al-Fitr*, people knock on the doors of neighbors, greeting them with the phrase *"Eid Mubarak"* (Blessed *Eid*). Friends or relatives living away are sent *Eid* greeting cards (left).

Eid *greeting card*

Stained glass panel

'ID BALLOONS
Colorful balloons are a popular feature of the celebrations of *'Id al-Fitr*, which marks the end of Ramadan (p. 15). Celebrations include a festival prayer, a substantial breakfast, and the giving of alms to the poor.

THE ISLAMIC CALENDAR

MUHARRAM	SAFAR	RABI' AL-AWWAL
The sacred month, 30 days	The month which is void	The first spring
1: *Ra's al-'Am* (New Year)	29 days	30 days
10: *Ashura*		12: Mawlid an-Nabi (birthday of the Prophet)

SALLAH FESTIVAL
Some Muslim festivals are local celebrations that take part in just one country or region of the Islamic world. For example, the *Sallah* festival is held in northern Nigeria as part of the rituals marking the end of Ramadan. The highlight is a colorful procession featuring chiefs in ceremonial robes, brightly costumed horsemen, and lute players.

ASHURA
The festival of *Ashura* marks the death of Husayn and, in one of the ceremonies, models of Husayn's tomb are carried through the streets. Plays reenacting the death of Husayn may also be performed.

WHIRLING DERVISH
Members of the Sufi Mevlevi order (p. 35) hold festivals at which they perform their "whirling" dance, known as *sama'*. One such festival marks the death of their founder, the great Sufi poet and mystic, Jalaluddin Rumi (1207–73).

WEDDING CELEBRATIONS
In Islam, a contract of marriage is made by the groom giving the bride-to-be a dowry, and the bride then giving consent to marriage before witnesses. The dowry may be presented in an embroidered wallet. Wedding celebrations vary according to the local traditions of the different areas of the Muslim world, but will usually include recitations from the Qur'an and a great feast.

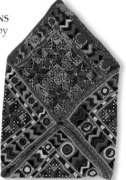

Dowry wallet

KHITAN
Muslim boys are usually circumcised in a ceremony called *khitan*. This is often done around age seven, though it may be done any time before a boy reaches 12 years old. These Turkish boys are attending a mosque before their *khitan* ceremony.

LAYLAT AL-ISRA' WA'L-MI'RAJ
On the 27th day of the month of *Rajab*, Muslims celebrate Muhammad's Night Journey, when he rode the beast called the *Buraq*, and his Ascension to Heaven (p. 9). This is called *Laylat al-Isra' wa'l-mi'raj*, the Night of the Journey and Ascension.

The Buraq is a "miraculous steed," although depictions of the beast vary.

RABI'ATH-THANI	JUMADA-L-ULA	JUMADA-TH-THANIYYAH
The second spring	The first month of dryness	The second month of dryness
29 days	30 days	29 days

61

Continued on next page

CANDY TRAY
The availability of sugar meant that many Muslim areas developed their own traditional types of candy. These examples come from Malaysia. Known as *kuch*, they are rich cookies flavored with palm sugar and coconut.

Food

A rich variety of food originated in the Islamic countries, and many of these foods have spread far and wide. This variety is only slightly limited by some simple dietary rules that restrict what a Muslim may eat. Islam forbids the drinking of alcohol, and Muslims are not allowed to eat pork which, as in other traditions, is considered to be unclean. Other animals may be eaten, provided that they are slaughtered in the correct way, with the Name of God pronounced as the creature's life is taken. Meat that is slaughtered in this way is described as *halal*, or lawful to eat.

MINT TEA
Tea is widely drunk in many Muslim countries. Usually served in a glass, hot, sweet mint tea is very popular and refreshing. Lemon tea is a common alternative.

Cardamom   Cumin

Turmeric

SPICES
The spice trade was always important to Muslim merchants, so many spices from India and Southeast Asia found their way into the cooking of the Middle East. Ingredients such as cumin and cardamom were valued for their fragrance, flavor and as aids to digestion.

ON SALE
This mother and daughter in Isfahan, Iran, are buying food from a local dealer in dried fruit and spices. In this traditional shop, most of the goods are displayed loose, so that purchasers can see exactly what they are buying.

FAST FOOD
The idea of fast, ready-to-eat food is nothing new in the Islamic world, and street sellers cooking and selling their own food are a common sight. In Egypt, street vendors like this man sell passersby fava bean patties cooked in the open air and flavored with local herbs.

DATE PALM
Date palms are one of the few crops that grown all over the dry areas of western Asia and northern Africa. Tasty and rich in carbohydrates, dates are a popular staple food.

RAJAB	SHA'BAN	RAMADAN
The revered month	The month of division	Month of great heat
30 days	29 days	30 days
27: *Laylat al-Mi'raj* (Night Journey)	15: *Laylat al-Bara'ah* (memory of the dead – Iran and India)	27: *Laylat al-Qadr* (Night of the Descent of the Qur'an)

FOR THE SWEET TOOTH
Sweet pastries are one of the delights of western Asia. This shop is in Syria. It is selling local pastries called *hama*, which get their sweetness from a covering of honey. Several different varieties are displayed in the shop window to tempt passersby.

BREADMAKER
Unleavened bread – bread baked without yeast, so that it stays flat and does not rise – is a common staple food throughout the Islamic world. This woman in Kyrgyzstan is making it on an open fire, which is one of the traditional ways to bake bread. Bread like this may also be baked on a hot stone.

LAMB KEBOBS
The technique of grilling small pieces of meat on a skewer to make a kebob is used in the eastern Mediterranean and Turkey. Kebobs made with ground lamb, cubes of lamb, or pieces of chicken, are now popular all over Europe and beyond.

ORANGES
Oranges came to Europe along trade routes from the Islamic world, and their juices were quenching thirsts in Western Europe by about the 14th century. The very term orange is derived from the Arabic word *naranj*.

COFFEE POT
Another item introduced to the West by the Muslims is coffee. Excellent coffee has been grown for centuries in the southwestern corner of the Arabian Peninsula and is still served there today, usually very strong and sweet, from elegant pots like this.

SHARING A MEAL
Hospitality has always been a virtue in Islam, especially in the desert, where food is hard to come by. This early illustration shows some Persians sharing food with a stranger.

FAMILY FOOD
This family in Senegal is cooking their meal over an open fire. When it is ready, they will all eat the food from the one pot. Everyone looks forward to this daily family gathering. It is a chance to catch up on the news as well as to enjoy a welcome meal.

SHAWWAL
The month of hunting
29 days
1: *'Id al-Fitr* (Feast of Fast-breaking)

DHU L-QA'DAH
The month of rest
30 days

DHU L-HIJJAH
Month of the Pilgrimage
29 days (sometimes 30)
10: *'Id al-Adha* (Feast of Sacrifice)

Did you know

FASCINATING FACTS

Historians believe chess was invented in India, but the first known mention of the game is in an ancient Islamic poem. By the 8th century, it was so popular in Persia that chess championships were held in the caliph's palace.

Tales of Sindbad the Sailor, Ali Baba and the Forty Thieves, and Aladdin and his Magic Lantern all originated in *The Arabian Nights*, a collection of Islamic stories that has been around since the 9th century.

Sinbad carried by an eagle

Illustration from *The Arabian Nights*

The trade and cultivation of coffee originated in the Islamic world. Coffee beans were traded from the town of Mocha, which has given its name to a strong, rich brew. People drank coffee not only at home but also in coffeehouses, where they could chat, listen to music, or catch up with the day's news.

The Chinese showed their trading partners in the Islamic world how to make paper. But Muslims used linen rather than mulberry bark as the raw material, an innovation that led to better paper. Islamic paper was regarded as the finest in the world. It was also very difficult to erase marks on linen paper, cutting down on forgeries.

How did ancient Muslim farmers get water in a desert? Through qanats, an underground network of tunnels linking to a series of manholes. These tunnels, completely dug by hand, carried water from an aquifer to outlying areas. There are an incredible 22,000 qanats in Iran, covering 170,000 miles (273,588 km). Even more amazing is that most of them are still in use, even though they are thousands of years old.

Because ripe sesame pods burst open at the slightest touch, Scheherazade, the storyteller of *The Arabian Nights*, coined the phrase, "Open sesame!" In her stories, speaking those words could open any doors.

Muslims tell time by the moon, rather than the Sun. The day begins at sunset rather than dawn. This means, for example, that as the sun is setting on Friday, Saturday begins.

Pen-and-ink calligraphy

Early Islamic book

The Islamic skill in calligraphy means that many books are works of art. In fact, a great calligrapher is given the same acclaim as a painter and sculptor might receive in the West.

Once paper was made, Muslim traders developed a paper-based economy. The old Persian word for an order for payment, *saak*, is the origin of our word, "check."

Backgammon is still a popular game in Muslim countries.

Backgammon is an ancient board game, first played 5,000 years ago in Mesopotamia. Players used stones as markers and dice made of stones, bones, wood, or pottery on a wooden playing board very similar to modern boards.

The tower of La Giralda in Seville, Spain, built by Islamic architects in the 12th century may have been Europe's first observatory. The tower, which also was used as a minaret, brought Islamic astronomers 305 feet (93 m) closer to the heavenly bodies they were mapping!

Do you love algebra? Thank the ancient Muslims. This equation-based branch of mathematics gets its name from the Islamic word *al jabr*, which means "completion." The first known algebra book was published by a Muslim mathematician sometime in the 11th century.

Windmills were used in Persia as early as the 7th century B.C.E. They did not appear in Europe until the 12th century, after European crusaders had made contact with the Muslims.

Muhammad is said to have adored cats. One legend says he cut off the sleeve of his garment when it was time to go to prayer rather than disturb his cat, who was napping on it. Some people say the distinctive "M" on a tabby cat's forehead is there as a lasting sign of Muhammad's affection for cats.

The Detroit suburb of Dearborn, MI is home to the second-largest Muslim population outside of the Middle East; Paris, France has the largest.

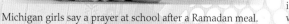
Michigan girls say a prayer at school after a Ramadan meal.

QUESTIONS AND ANSWERS

Q Is Islam the oldest of the world's major religions?

A No. It is the youngest of the three great monotheistic (the belief that there is only one God) religions. The other two, Christianity and Judaism, are older.

Q How large is the world's Muslim population?

A Latest estimates place the number of people who follow Islam worldwide at 1.7 billion—about one in five people on the planet. Christianity is the largest religion, but Islam is the fastest-growing faith.

Q Which nation has the largest Muslim population?

A There are some 200 million Muslims in Indonesia. This represents about 85 percent of the total population.

Q How many Muslims live in the United States of America?

A It is very difficult to estimate the number of American Muslims. The U.S. Constitution prohibits questions about religion in the census. Some studies report figures of between one and two million; others give numbers of between six and seven million.

Q How many mosques are there in the United States?

A There are over 1,200 mosques in the United States. More than 60 percent were founded after 1980.

Q Which states have the largest Muslim populations?

A Again, it is difficult to estimate this figure with accuracy. We do know that these states have the largest Muslim populations, in descending order: California, New York, Illinois, New Jersey, Indiana, Michigan, Virginia, Texas, Ohio, and Maryland.

Q What is the difference between the terms "Islam" and "Muslim?"

A "Islam" is the name for the religion itself, and "Muslim" is the name for a follower of Islam. It is the same thing as the difference between Christianity and a Christian. The adjective form of the religion is *Islamic*.

Thousands of pilgrims gather at Mecca.

Q What is the spiritual center of Islam?

A The spiritual heart of the Muslim world is in the Haram, the sacred enclosure in Mecca, the birthplace of Muhammed.

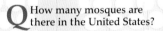

A 1,200-year-old Qur'an

Q What is the Qur'an? Is it the same as the Koran?

A The Quran, also known as the Koran, is the holy book of Islam containing the word of God. Throughout history, scholars have studied its teachings by making elaborate copies, which is why calligraphy became so developed in Islam.

Q Do all Muslims practice the same form of Islam?

A Not quite. About 90 percent of Muslims are Sunnis, who follow Muhammad's teachings. The other 10 percent are Shi'ite. The Shi'ites have developed different devotions and practices but both groups essentially practice the same religion.

Q What is a mosque?

A The place where Muslims gather to pray and worship is called a mosque. A tower called a minaret is a common feature to all mosques. Inside the mosque is a mihrab, a decorated niche in the wall that marks the direction of Mecca. The minbar is a pulpit to the right of the mihrab. There is a large, open area for people to pray in.

Q Who leads the prayer at a mosque?

A The imam leads the prayers and teaches people at a mosque. Religious authority in a Muslim community rests with the Qur'an, not with a person. There is nothing equivalent to a priesthood, since there are no sacraments. In a sense, every Muslim is his own "leader" because he or she must carry out the Five Pillars, the obligations of the religion.

Record breakers

☪ **LARGEST MOSQUE**
The enormous Shah Fiesal mosque in Islamabad, Pakistan can hold 100,000 people.

☪ **TALLEST MINARET**
The minaret at Shah Alum, Selangor, near Kuala Lumpur is 450 feet (137 m) tall.

☪ **OLDEST STANDING MINARET**
The minaret at the mosque in Kairouan, Tunisia was built in 728 C.E.

☪ **OLDEST MOSQUE**
The Ummayed Mosque in Damascus, Syria is believed to be the world's oldest mosque. It was completed in 705 C.E.

Sha Fiesal Mosque

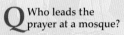

Timeline

Qur'an

Richly decorated leather cover

THE CHRONOLOGY OF THE HISTORY of Islam has a definite beginning: the birth of Muhammad. Within a few decades, the religion he founded, Islam, spread from the city of Mecca across the Arabian Peninsula. Armies bearing the word of Islam conquered an empire that eventually stretched east across northern Africa to the Atlantic coast of Spain, and west to the borders of China and India. Much of the history of Islam is marked by fierce fighting for control of West and Central Asia. Today, Islam is on the rise once again: it is the fastest-growing faith in the world.

570

Muhammad is born in the city of Mecca, in what is now Saudi Arabia. A member of the Quaraysh tribe, he was orphaned as a boy and brought up by relatives.

610

In seclusion on Mount Hira during a month-long retreat, Muhammad has his first revelation through the Angel Gabriel, who tells him that he is the Prophet of God. The holy book of Islam, the Qur'an, is also revealed to Muhammad.

622

The Islamic calendar begins when Muhammad and his followers are invited to move to the city that is now Media. This migration, known as the *hijira*, marks the start of the Islamic era.

630

Mecca is conquered by Muslim forces and becomes the spiritual center of Islam; today, it remains Islam's most sacred city.

632

The Prophet Muhammad dies, but the religion that he preached, Islam, continues to spread throughout the region.

632

Muhammad's father-in-law, Abu Bakr, becomes the first of the four caliphs—viceroys or successors—that are known as the Rightly Guided Caliphs.

633–42

Muslims conquer Syria, Iraq, and Egypt; Persia, modern-day Iran, also comes under Muslim rule.

669

The Arab conquest of North Africa extends beyond Tripoli to the west.

680

Arab armies advance to the Atlantic Ocean for the first time, at Morocco in Northern Africa.

687–692

Construction on the Dome of the Rock begins in Jerusalem; it is completed in 692. This mosque is built on the spot where Muhammad is said to have ascended to heaven, and it is the earliest example of Islamic architecture still standing.

696

Arabic becomes the official language of Islam.

697–698

The great North African city of Carthage, founded by the Phoenicians and later home to the Romans, falls to Muslim armies.

c. 751

The Arabs learn papermaking, possibly from captured Chinese prisoners. Their paper is soon regarded as the finest in the world.

762–765

Baghdad, a city on the Tigris River in present-day Iraq, is founded as a great center of arts and learning. A school of medicine is founded there in 765.

c. 800s

The Arabic number system using place value and zero is used by Muslims. Arab ships are reported sailing as far as China.

c. 900s

The most famous Islamic university, Cairo's al-Azhar University, is founded.

The exterior of the Dome of the Rock is decorated with calligraphy.

1090

The first mention of the Arabic use of compasses is printed in a Chinese book.

1095

Pope Urban II calls for a Christian army to capture Jerusalem; European armies begin planning the first of four crusades.

1096

European crusaders on the First Crusade reach Constantinople.

1099

French and Norman knights capture the city of Jerusalem.

1147

The Second Crusade; Lisbon is captured from the Moors.

1150

The Iraqi Sultan of Baghdad starts a postal service using carrier pigeons.

1150–1250

The crusader castle Krak des Chevaliers is built in Syria.

1187

Saladin, a Kurdish general and widely respected leader, defeats the Crusaders and takes Jerusalem.

1191

In the Third Crusade, King Richard I, Richard the Lion-hearted, recovers some of the territory taken by Saladin.

1193

Muslims begin their conquest of India. Saladin dies.

1204

Crusaders sack Constantinople.

1206

Genghis Khan leads the Mongols on a conquest of Central Asia.

1258

Mongol army sacks Baghdad and kills the caliph, devastating the political center of Islam.

1259

An observatory is set up in Persia. By the 13th century, Muslim scholars know a vast amount about astronomy.

1325

Legendary Muslim traveler Ibn Battuta begins his 29-year journey that will take him from Tangier, now Morocco, to West and East Africa, Arabia, India, and China.

Battle dress

Genghis Khan

1338–1390

The Alhambra is built in Spain.

1347

The Black Death reaches Baghdad and Constantinople.

1375

The great Muslim historian Ibn Khaldun begins his work, the *Muqaddima.*

1453

Ottoman Turks conquer Constantinople and name it Istanbul; they soon spread their empire through the Middle East.

1498

Vasco de Gama sails around the Cape of Good Hope to reach India.

1520

Suleyman the Magnificent begins his 46-year reign.

1575

At the height of the Ottoman empire, an observatory is founded at Galata, now part of Istanbul, Turkey.

1653

The Taj Mahal is completed in India as a mausoleum for Mughal Shah Jehan's wife. More than 20,000 laborers worked for 20 years to complete what is regarded as the crown jewel in Islamic architecture.

1672

The Ottoman Empire reaches its greatest extent.

1869

The Suez Canal is completed. This canal joins the Mediterranean Sea and the Red Sea via the Gulf of Suez for the first time, opening a new shipping route.

1919

The End of World War I leads to the formation of the League of Nations. The Ottoman Empire is broken into smaller states, each of which are placed under the control of France or Great Britain.

1924

Turkey's first president, Kemal Ataturk, abolishes the caliphate in a bid to modernize the country.

1947

Pakistan is created from India to meet the demand for a mostly Muslim state.

1952

The McCarren-Walter act relaxes U.S. ban on Asian immigration; large numbers of Muslim students come to the United States.

1957

The Islamic Center opens in Washington, D.C. The center contains a mosque as well as an extensive library collection.

1960s

Wave of Islamic immigration from the Middle East: Indian and Pakistani peoples move to Great Britain; Northern Africans move to France; Turks move to Germany.

1962

Algeria gains its independence from France after an eight-year civil war.

1965

Changes in U.S. laws enable working professionals (for example, doctors and engineers) from Pakistan, Bangladesh, and Saudi Arabia into the United States, helping to establish the Islamic faith here.

1979

The Iranian Revolution re-establishes the Islamic Republic of Iran, the first attempt at an Islamic state in the modern era.

1988

In Pakistan, Benazir Bhutto, the daughter of a former Prime Minister, is sworn in as the first female Prime Minister of a Muslim nation; the Iran-Iraq war ends.

Mongol raiding party

1990

Dr. Shirin Tahir-Kheli becomes the first Muslim U.S. ambassador to the UN.

1990s

Islamic fundamentalism is on the rise.

1993

Islamic countries issue Cairo Declaration to curb fundamentalism.

2004

Robina Muqimyar is the first woman in Afghanistan's history to compete in the Olympic Games.

Find out more

ISLAMIC FAITH AND CULTURE are often in the news, but they are still sometimes misunderstood. Here is a guide to learning more about the faith, history, and traditions of Islam, past and present. A good way to begin is a visit to your local mosque or Islamic center. Mosques function as information centers for the local Muslim community, so you will be able to find out about special events in your area. Many Islamic center libraries are also open to the public. You can find books related to Islam at your local library. Several museums in the United States have strong collections of Islamic art, from tiles to textiles.

Abstract design

VISIT A MUSEUM'S ISLAMIC COLLECTION
Because of the prohibition of the depiction of humans and animals, Islamic art developed its own distinctive traditions. Its primary forms—geometric, arabesque, floral, and calligraphic—are often used together. Pay a visit to the Islamic hall of an art museum such as the Los Angeles County Museum of Art (above) to see these forms as represented in painting, architecture, books, and the decorative arts.

ISLAMIC ART
This beautiful star-shaped tile creates an immediate impact with its strong color and interesting design. Because so many mosques are tiled inside and out, tilemaking is a highly-developed art in the Muslim world.

CALLIGRAPHY
Pens like these were used to create Islamic calligraphy. If you would like to try your hand at this ancient art, check with your local art museum or try the Internet to find a list of nearby classes.

Stylized decoration based on geometric and floral designs

USEFUL WEB SITES

- A site for non-Muslims who want to understand Islam:
  www.islamicweb.com
- A portal to information on Islam and the Muslim community:
  www.islamicfinder.org
- An independent, multi-faith online community:
  www.beliefnet.com
- A huge Web site providing a guide to Islam, past and present:
  www.islamfortoday.com/shia.htm
- Explore Muslim heritage through an interactive timeline:
  www.muslimheritage.com/timeline/default.cfm
- Hear how each letter in the Arabic alphabet is pronounced:
  http://abcsofarabic.tripod.com/alphabetpage.htm
- An excellent overview of ancient Islamic history:
  www.wsu.edu/~dee/islam/islam.htm
- A site to help put today's news from the Middle East into perspective:
  www.pbs.org/wgbh/globalconnections/mideast/index.html
- An inside look at the pilgrimage and its role in Islam:
  www.cnn.com/specials/2002/hajj
- Companion site to PBS Frontline documentary on Muslims:
  www.pbs.org/wgbh/frontline/shows/muslims

INSIDE A MOSQUE
Many mosques have plain and simple exteriors, with lavishly decorated interiors. All mosques contain a mirhab, a niche in the wall that shows the direction of Mecca. This horseshoe-shaped arch over a mirhab in Crodoba, Spain is a beautiful example of Islamic architectural style.

EXPLORING ISLAMIC CULTURE

Ask at your local Islamic Center or check the Internet or newspaper listings for Islamic festivals or cultural events in your area. You might learn to write your name in calligraphy, hear traditional music, try different traditional foods, or see a dance performance. These dancers on the island of Korcula in Croatia are performing the traditional Moreska dance. This colorful dance, performed as far back as 1156, tells the story of a Muslim and Christian encounter during the age of the Crusades.

Places to Visit

BROOKLYN MUSEUM OF ART, BROOKLYN, NEW YORK
This museum's collection from Iran's Qajar dynasty is the only one of its kind in the United States.

DETROIT INSTITUTE OF ARTS, DETROIT, MICHIGAN
This important collection of Islamic decorative art is especially strong in the art of the book

METROPOLITAN MUSEUM OF ART, NEW YORK, NEW YORK
One of the most comprehensive collections of Islamic art anywhere, this collection contains nearly 12,000 objects from as far west as Spain and Morocco and as far east as India and Central Asia.

LOS ANGELES COUNTY MUSEUM OF ART, LOS ANGELES, CALIFORNIA
This museum's permanent collection features Islamic art from the 7th through 19th centuries.

CLEVELAND MUSEUM OF ART, CLEVELAND, OHIO
This collection contains a beautiful mosaic mihrab from Iran.

ARTHUR M. SACKLER MUSEUM AT HARVARD UNIVERSITY, CAMBRIDGE, MASSACHUSETTS
This small but important collection of 2,500 works features pottery, textiles, and lacquers, and is particularly strong in paintings.

New York's Brooklyn Bridge

ISLAM IN AMERICA

Of Muslims in the United States today, about two-thirds brought their religion with them as immigrants from other countries. The other third, mostly African Americans, were born in America. By 2015, Islam is expected to be the second-largest religion in America; this number alone provides a compelling reason to find out more about Islam.

Message from the Qur'an on a mosque wall

ISLAMIC CULTURAL CENTER

The Islamic Cultural Center in Washington, D.C., is the largest mosque in the United States. On Friday afternoons, traffic on Massachusetts Avenue comes almost to a standstill as hundreds flock to the mosque for prayers. Although non-Muslims may not attend prayers, the mosque and its library welcome visitors at other times. Remember to show respect whenever you are in a place of worship.

ISLAM IN THE MOVIES

Muslims may be misrepresented in movies, leaving non-followers misguided. Spike Lee's 1992 movie *Malcolm X*, a portrait of the civil rights leader and his conversion to Islam, provided a more balanced view.

Glossary

ADHAN The call to prayer; often made by a muezzin

'ASR The late afternoon prayer

ALGEBRA A mathematical system in which letters or other symbols are used to stand for numbers

ALLAH The name of the one God in whom Muslims believe and upon whom all life and all existence depends

ALMSGIVING The giving of gifts to the poor and needy; one form of almsgiving, zakat, is one of the Five Pillars of Islam

ANATOLIA A largely mountainous plateau occupying the peninsula between the Black Sea, the Mediterranean, and the Aegean

ARABIA A peninsula in southwest Asia between the Red Sea and the Persian Gulf

ARABS Semitic people originally of the Arabian Peninsula, now widespread throughout southwest Asia and northern Africa

ASTROLABE An instrument once used to find the altitude of a star or other heavenly body

ASTRONOMY The science of the stars, planets, and all other heavenly bodies, which studies their composition, motion, relative position, and size

BAGHDAD Former caliphate city in southwest Asia; on the Tigris River in present-day Iraq

BATIK A decorative method of dyeing cloth using wax

BEDOUIN Peoples of the nomadic desert tribes of Arabia, Syria, or northern Africa

BERBERS Pre-Arab inhabitants of North Africa. Berbers were scattered in tribes across the mountains and deserts of Morocco, Algeria, Tunisia, Libya, and Egypt.

BYZANTINE EMPIRE The eastern part of the Roman Empire, with its capital at Byzantium, present-day Constantinople

CALIPH The title taken by Mohammad's successors as the secular and religious leaders of Islam

CALIPHATE The rank or reign of a caliph; the lands ruled by a caliph

CALLIGRAPHY Decorative, stylized writing, practiced as an art

CARAVAN A company of travelers, especially merchants or pilgrims, traveling together for safety

CONQUEST The act of taking possession of something after winning a war

CONSTANTINOPLE The ancient city that was the capital of the east Roman Empire until its capture by the Ottomans; now Istanbul

CRUSADES A series of campaigns by western European Christian armies to recapture the Holy Land from the Muslims

DAMASCUS An ancient city in Syria

DHIMMIS Non-Muslims living in Islamic regions whose rights are protected by the state

DHOW A single-masted ship with a triangular sail, sharp prow, and raised deck at the stern

DOME OF THE ROCK A mosque in Jerusalem; the earliest example of Islamic architecture still standing

FAJR the first prayer of the day, before sunrise

Minarets make a stunning skyline

Minarets in the skyline of Cairo, Egypt

FASTING To abstain from all or certain foods

FIVE PILLARS OF ISLAM The five fundamental requirements of practicing Islam. The Pillars are iman, salah, zakat, sawm, and hajj.

FRANKINCENSE A gum resin obtained from trees in Arabia and Northeast Africa; burned as incense

GABRIEL The archangel; the messenger of God who revealed the Qur'an to Muhammad

HADITH An account of the prophet Muhammad's life; a collection of Muhammads sayings

HAFIZ A person who has committed the text of the Qur'an to memory

HAJJ The pilgrimage to the Islamic holy city of Mecca in Saudi Arabia. It includes a series of rites over several days and is one of the Five Pillars of Islam.

HALAL Food that is lawful for Muslims to eat under their dietary rules

HIJAB The veil worn by some Muslim women

HIJRAH Muhammad's migration from Mecca to Medina in 622, which marks the beginning of the Muslim era and calendar

HOLY LAND A general name for Palestine and Israel

IHRAM the special state of holiness pilgrims must achieve before a pilgrimage; the special clothing worn on a pilgrimage to Mecca

IKAT A technique that involves tie-dyeing threads before weaving to create bold, colorful fabric

IMAM A prayer leader

Bedouin travelers in a caravan

IMAN Faith; one of the Five Pillars of Islam

INDIGO A blue dye made from plants

'ISHA the last prayer of the day, in the evening

ISLAM A monotheistic religion founded by the Prophet Muhammad; its name means "submission" and comes from the word for "peace."

JABAL AN-NUR The Mountain of Light; the place near Mecca where Muhammad went to meditate. The Qur'an was first revealed to him here.

JULUS A stage in Muslim prayer; the sitting position

KHANJARA Type of sharp dagger used as a personal weapon

KHUTBA The name for a sermon delivered by an imam

KUFIC A bold, angular style of script used in Islamic calligraphy

KURSI A wooden support for holding a copy of the Qur'an

MAGHRIB the fourth prayer of the day, after sunset

MECCA The birthplace of Muhammad; Islam's holiest city and a center of pilgrimage; in present-day Saudi Arabia

MEDINA Muhammad's capital city in present-day Saudi Arabia; the site of his tomb

MIHRAB An often elaborate niche in the wall of a mosque indicating the direction to Mecca

MINARET The highest point of a mosque, from which the call to prayer is given

MINBAR A raised pulpit in a mosque where the imam stands to give a sermon

MONGOLS Nomadic people of Central Asia who made many conquests from the 13th century onward

MOSQUE In Islam, the place of worship; a building specifically used for prayer and open for prayer throughout the week

Intricately carved mosque doors

MUSHAF Literally, a collection of pages; a copy of the Qur'an

MUHAMMAD Prophet and founder of Islam, born in Mecca, to whom Gabriel revealed messages from God. These were written down in the Qur'an.

MUEZZIN In Islam, the person who sounds the call to prayer

MULLAH A person who is learned in religion. Most mullahs have had formal religious training.

Prayer mat with mosque design

NOMAD A member of a tribe or people which has no permanent home, but moves about constantly

OASIS A fertile place in a desert due to a source of water

OTTOMAN EMPIRE Islamic empire established in Anatolia in the late 13th century

PERSIA The name for the Middle Eastern nation that is now Iran

PILGRIMAGE *See* hajj

PRAYER MAT A small rug used by many followers of Islam for prayer

QIBLA The direction to Mecca. Muslims pray in this direction.

QUADRANT An instrument for measuring altitudes in astronomy and navigation

QUR'AN The holy book of Islam; the word of God, as revealed to Muhammad. This name usually refers to the book that has the Qur'an written in it; originally, it referred to the words themselves, which Muslims had to learn by heart.

RAK'A In Muslim prayer, the motion of bowing down to show respect for Allah

SALAH The regular daily prayers in Islam said five times a day; one of the Five Pillars of Islam

SALAM The final stage in daily prayer; the peace

SAWM The name for the fast during the month of Ramadan; one of the Five Pillars of Islam.

SELJUKS Nomadic Turkish peoples who began to spread southwards in the 11th century, capturing Baghdad

SHAHADA In Islam, a profession of faith

SHARIA The name for the holy law of Islam compiled and codified in the 8th and 9th centuries

SURA One of the 114 chapters in the Qur'an, the holy book

TIRAZ Specially made cloth woven with calligraphic designs

TURKS A general name for central Asian peoples of nomadic origin

WAQF A gift given to the state for good works such as building a mosque

Zakat is usually paid with cash

ZAKAT A tax that is paid as a percentage of a person's wealth, which is distributed among the poor and needy; one of the Five Pillars of Islam

ZUHR the noon prayer; on Fridays, Muslim men are required to gather for the midday prayer.

Index

A

Abraham 17
Adam 17
Africa 23, 48-49
Akbar 45, 53
'Ali 20, 21
al-Idrisi 28
Allah 9, 10, 12, 13
almsgiving 12, 14, 19
Arab Empire 22
Arabia 6-7
Arabian Nights 27
Arabic: numbers 31;
  script *see* script, Arabic
Arabs 6
Ashura 60, 61
astronomy 24, 29
Ataturk 21
Avicenna 24

B C

Babur 53
Baghdad 20, 28, 29, 50
Bedouin people 33, 56
Boabdil 47
Buraq 9, 61
Byzantine Empire 7, 22
calendar, Muslim 60-63
caliphs, caliphate 20-21
calligraphy 8, 26, 27, 48
camels 33, 39, 55;
  caravans 8, 21, 38, 40

caranvanserai 36, 55
Carthage 23
ceremonies 60-61
China 54-55, 57
Christians 12, 42, 46, 58
circumcision 61
cities 36-37; walls 37
Constantinople *see*
  Istanbul
Cordoba 46
costume 17, 48, 56-57
crusades 42-43

D F

Damascus 22, 40
dhows 39
dietary rules 62
dowry 59, 61
faith *see* Shahada
family life 58-59
fasting 12, 15
festivals 15, 60-61
Five Pillars of Islam 12-17
food 15, 41, 62-63
France 23
frankincense 7, 40

G H I

Gabriel, archangel 8, 9,
  10, 17
Genghis Khan 50
God, One *see* Allah
government, Muslim 58
Granada 47; Alhambra
  46, 47; Generalife 47

hajj 16
halal meat 62
houses 17, 32
Husayn 21, 60
Ibn Battuta 38
Ibn Sina 24, 30
'Id al-Adha 60
'Id al-Fitr 15, 60
ikat 35, 57
iman 12
India 52, 53
Indonesia 54
Iran 52
Isfahan 52
Islam, basic belief 12
Islamic: art/decoration
  11, 20, 26, 34-35, 53; city
  36-37; culture 34-35
Istanbul 51: Blue Mosque
  19; Hagia Sofia 51;
  observatory 29;
  Topkapi Palace 34

J K L

Jerusalem 22, 42, 43;
  Temple Mount 9
jewelry 56-57
Jews/Judaism 12, 42, 58
Ka'ba 16, 17; Black Stone
  17
Kerbala 60
Khadija 8
Khalifa 20
khanjar 45
khitan 61
khutba 12, 19
Krak des Chevaliers 43

Kublai Khan 50, 54
law, Muslim, *see* sharia
learning 24, 28
libraries 18, 25

M

madrasah 24
Mali 48, 49
Mamluks 43, 50
Ma'rib 7
markets 32, 36
marriage 59, 61
Martel, Charles 23
mathematics 31
Mawlid an-Nabi 60
Mecca 13, 16, 17; Sacred
  Mosque 16
medicine 30-31, 36
Medina 9
Mehmet II 51
men 59
merchants 8, 32, 38-41, 54,
  55
metalwork 34, 47, 52, 57
mihrab 13, 18
minarets 12, 18, 48, 52
minbar 12
Mongols 20, 33, 50-51, 52
Moors 46
mosques 18-19, 22, 48, 54,
  55
muezzin 12
Mughal Empire 53
Muhammad, Prophet 8-9,
  10, 20
mullah 25
music, Arab 35, 46

N O P Q

Night Journey 60, 61
Night of Destiny 8
nomads 6, 32-33
oases 6, 7, 32
observatories 29
Ottomans 19, 50
pharmacists 30, 31
pilgrimage to Mecca 13,
  16-17
pilgrims 16, 17, 42
poetry 25
prayer 12-13, 15, 18, 59;
  call to 12, 18; direction
  of 13; stages of 13
Prophet of Islam, The *see*
  Muhammad
prophets 8
public baths/fountains
  14, 37
Qur'an 8, 10-11, 25, 34;
  copying out/writing
  down 8, 11, 48;
  memorizing 8, 49;
  wearing 49

R S

Ramadan 8, 10, 15, 60
Richard the Lionheart 43
Saladin (Salah-ad-Din) 43
scholars 24-27, 28
schools 24, 26, 56
script: Arabic 9, 10, 26,
  27; Kufic 10; South
  Arabic 6

Shahada 12
sharia 58
Shi'i Muslims 20, 21,
  52, 60
Silk Road 38, 39, 40
society 58-59
soldiers 23, 50
Southeast Asia 54-55
Spain 22, 23, 46-47
spices 41, 62
Sufism 35, 61
sugar 41, 62
Sunni 20, 21
suqs 36

T U W Y Z

tents 17, 33
Timur (Tamerlane) 50, 52
tombs 9, 24, 49, 52
trade/traders 6, 8, 32, 38-
  41, 54
trade routes 6, 7, 38, 39
travelers 38-41
Turks 12, 44, 50-51
universities, Islamic 24
waqf 14, 18
weapons 42, 44-45
wedding/brides 56, 57,
  59, 61
whirling dervishes 35, 61
women 55, 56, 59
writing 26-27;
  ink/inkwells 25, 26, 27,
  34; pens/brushes 26,
  27, 34; set/box 25, 34
Yemen 6, 7, 32
zakat 14

Acknowledgments

The publisher would like to thank: Philip Letsu and Wilfrid Wood for design assistance.

The author would like to thank: Batul Salazar for correcting errors and mistakes of judgment, and for sharing knowledge and sources of information with such generosity and good humor.

Picture Credits
Key: a=above, b=below, c=center, l=left, r=right, t=top; Abbreviations: **BAL:** Bridgeman Art Library, London/New York; **CO:** Christine Osborne; **DKPL:** DK Picture Library; **PS:** Peter Sanders; **C:** Corbis; **RHPL:** Robert Harding Picture Library; **V&A:** Victoria and Albert Museum, London; **SHP:** Sonia Halliday Photographs; **HL:** Hutchison Library; **PP:** Panos Pictures.

1 Ancient Art & Architecture Collection: c. 2 Bodleian Library, University of Oxford: bc. BAL: Giraudon tr; Giraudon/ Topkapi Palace Museum, Istanbul tl. PS: tc. 3 AKG London: bl. C: tl. DKPL: Glasgow Museums. CO: c. 4 BAL: cr, crb, bc; Stapleton Collection cr. Werner Forman Archive: crb. Sanderson: bl. 5 DKPL: Ashmolean tr. 6 C: Araldo de Luca br; Paul Almasy bl. DKPL: British Museum br. PS: cl. Photograph by Paul Lunde: tr. 7 C: Archivo Iconografico br. DKPL: British Museum tr. 8 DKPL: British Museum tl. Impact Photos: Alan Keohane cr. Salazar: bl. PS: cl, bc. 9 AKG London: br. British Museum, London tr. Salazar: cl. PS: bl. 10 BAL: Musee Conde, Chantilly, France: 10-11. DKPL: British Library cl, bl. 11 DKPL: Ashmolean tr; British Library cr; Glasgow Museum cr. Private Collection: bl. 12 BAL: Stapleton collection tl, bc. PS: cl. 13 DKPL: National Maratime Museum tc. PS: c, c, cr, bl. 14 Photograph by Alexander Stone Lunde: cr. Private Collection: bl 15 AKG London: cr. HL: John Egan br. PS: cl. Nomad, King's

Parade, Cambridge: tr. 16 Private Collection: tl. PS: bl (both) 16-17 V&A: c. 17 BAL: Insititue of Oriental Studies, St Petersburg, Russia bc. Salazar: bl. Photograph by Paul Lunde: br. 18 CO: br. Private Collection: tl. Photograph by Alexander Stone Lunde: bl. 19 BAL: tc. CO: cr. V&A: tr. 20 BAL: Kunsthistorisches Meseum, Vienna, Austria br; Stapleton Collection bl. DKPL: Ashmolean c; British Museum: 20-21. 21 AKG London: br. BAL: Le Tresor de L@ Abbaye de Saint-Maurice, France tl; Stapleton Collection bl. PS: cb. V&A: tr. 22 Photograph by Paul Lunde: bl. C: Roger Wood br. The Art Archive: Archaeological Museum, Madrid tl. SHP: Jane Taylor br. Impact Photos: Jerry Flynn cr. 23 BAL: Volubilis, Morocco tl. Monasterio de El Escorial, Spain bl. C: Archivo Iconografico br. Archivo Fotgrafico: br. 24 BAL: bl; Louvre, Paris cr; Museo Real Academia de Medicina, Madrid tr. CO: br. 25 BAL: bl; Topkapi Palace Museum, Istanbul, Turkey br. CO: cr. Private Collection: tl, tr. 26 British Library, London tr. C: Adam Woolfit cr. British Library: 26-27 RHPL: David Beatty tl. 27 BAL: Royal Asiastic Society, London bc. DKPL: British Library tl. Mary Evans Picture Library: br. V&A: tr 28 Bodleian Library, University of Oxford: c. BAL: British Library tr. CO: bl. 29 BAL: Topkapi Palace Museum, Istanbul, Turkey br: University Library, Istanbul, Turkey tl. DKPL: National Maritime Museum cr. CO: tr. 30 BAL: Bibliotheque Nationale, Paris, France tl; Eton College, Windsor tr; Institute of Oriental Studies, St Petersburg, Russia bl. DKPL: Science Museum br. 31 DKPL: Museum of the Royal Pharmaceutical Society cb; Science Museum r. Werner Forman Archive: ct; Oriental Collection, State University Library, Leiden tl. James Stone Lunde: br. 32 BAL: tr. C: Abbie Enock: Travel Ink cl; Charles and Josette Lenars 32-33. CO: tl. PS: tl. 33 DKPL: Barnabas Kindersley cl. 34 Ahuzan Gallery, Ahuzan Islamic Art, London: c BAL: tr. DKPL: Aditya Patankar bl. John Gillow: br.

35 Bodleian Library, University of Oxford: cl. DKPL: Glasgow Museum br. BAL: Egyptian National Library, Cairo, Egypt cr. John Gillow: tr. 36 Panos Pictures: D. Sanson c. Private Collection: clb. 37 BAL: British Library, London tl. SHP: 1840 Engraving by Thomas Allom, hand painted by Laura Lushington cl. CO: r. 38 BAL: Institute of Oriental Studies, St. Petersberg, Russia tr. DKPL: National Maritime Museum 38-39; Royal Museum of Scotland cl. Mary Evans Picture Library: tl. CO: bl. 39 DKPL: David Gower tc. SHP: Topkapi Palace Museum cr. PS: tr. 40 DKPL: British Library cr; Natural History Museum tr, Pitt Rivers Museum bl. CO: tr. Property of Nomad, Kings Parade, Cambridge: c. John Gillow: cb. 41 James Stone Lunde: br. 42 BAL: Bibliotheque Nationale tl; Bibliotheque nationale, Paris cl. C: Dave G.Houser b. 43 AKG London: tr. Bonhams, London br; British Library, London cr; BritishLibrary, London bc. CO: cl. 44 DKPL: Arbour Antiques 44-45; Pitt Rivers Museum c. SHP: tl. Photograph by Alexander Stone Lunde: bl. V&A: c, 44-45. 45 BAL: tc, tr; Bargello Museum, Florence l. James Stone Lunde: cla. 46 BAL: Louvre, Paris, France cr; Monasterio de El Escorial, Spain c. Adam Woolfit tr; John Hesletine 46-47. DKPL: British Museum tl. Archivo Fotgrafico: br. C: cl; Edifice bc; Michael Busselle tr; Ric Ergenbright tl. 47 HL: Juliet Highet c. 48 AKG London: c. CO: tl. PP: Marcus Rose 48-49. O. Clasen: tr, Paul Lunde: bl. 49 C: Gerard Degeorge tr. DKPL: Pavillion Musem and Art Galleries tl. Fotomas Index: cr. PS: cl, br. 50 AKG London: tl. BAL: cl, br; British Museum bl. 51 BAL: tr, bl. The Art Archive: Topkapi Musuem, Istanbul br. SHP: c. 52 C: Paul Almasy b; Sheldan Collins cr. DKPL: Ashmolean tl, cl, C. 53 AKG London: V&A tr, cl. 54 CO: tl. John Gillow: tr. PS: cr, bl, bc. 55 C: Janet Wishnetsky br. RHPL: David Holdsworth tr. CO: bl. PS: cr. James Stone Lunde: tl. Private Collection: c. 56 RHPL: F Jack Jackson l. PS: tr, bc. 56-57 Property of Nomad, Kings Parade, Cambridge: c (robes and hat). 57 Sudhir Kasilwal: cr Property of Nomad, Kings Parade, Cambridge: tl. 58 BAL: Biblioteca Monasterio del Escorial, Madrid, Spain cr; Bibliotheque Nationale, Paris c. C: Earl & Nazima Kowall bl. SHP: tl. Panos

Pictures: Marc Schlossman br. Science Photo Library: Erich Schrempp tr. 59 RHPL; Bruno Morandi c; David Poole br PP: Clive Shirley tl; Liba Taylor bl; Piers Benatar tr. Salazar: cr. PS: cl. Baroness Udin/Universal Pictorial Press: clb. 60 CO: tr, cb. PS: c, br. Property of Nomad, King's Parade, Cambridge: br. 61 RHPL: Adam Woolfitt cl; J H C Wilson tr. HL,: tl. PP; Mark McEvoy bl. Property of John Gillow: cr. Collection Ali Bellagha: br, 62 A-Z Botanical Collection: Matt Johnston bl. PP: Trygve Bolstad cr. 63 BAL: British Library, London bl. DKPL: David Murray & Jules Selmes cl. RHPL: Christopher Rennie tl. HL: Sarah Errington tr. James Stone Lunde: c. PP: Jeremy Hartley br.

AP Wideworld Photos: 64bl, 65tr

Bridgeman Art Library: Illuminated pages of a Koran manuscript, Il-Khanid Mameluke School (vellum), Islamic School, (14th century) / Private Collection 65c

Corbis: Bettmann 64tl; Bureau L.A. Collection 69bl; Jason Florio 69c; Catherine Karnow 69br; Earl & Nazima Kowall 64c; Stapleton Collection 67tl; Keren Su 65br

DK: Max Alexander 64tl; Geoff Brightling 64br; Alistair Duncan 70tr, 70bl; Edinburgh University 67cl; Ellen Howdon 7t St Mungo, Glasgow Museums 68cr; Chas Howson, British Museum 71br; Barnabas Kindersley 71bl; Magnus Rew 66bl; Jon Spaull 70-71; Cecile Treal and Jean-Michel Ruiz 66tl, 66-67, 68-69 71t; Francesca York 64-65 Leandro Zoppe 65tl

Getty Images: Oleg Nikishin/Stringer 64tr

Front cover:
Tcl: National Maritime Museum, UK
Tcr: Glasgow Museums, UK
Tr: Ahuzan Gallery, Ahuzan Islamic Art, London
B: Steve Allen/Brand X Pictures/Alamy

Back cover:
Cl: Glasgow Museums, UK